In Every Moment remi
lives wherever we liv
"success" is, reading
suffered, Eva's stories

the field or a veteran, we can all relate to her global experiences. We may laugh or cry, but each lesson she learned becomes ours. We feel less alone, more understood, and encouraged that our stories matter. Her stories encourage us to follow God's leading to the world beyond or back home again.

— **Sue Eenigenburg**, co-author of *Expectations and Burnout, Sacred Siblings, Grit to Stay Grace to Go*

In Every Moment is a beautiful compilation of relatable devotional essays for the global worker that points our hearts back to the One who led us to these foreign shores. Eva Burkholder vulnerably shares personal stories from her own years on the field and invites us to see that the Lord is ever-working in the miraculous and the mundane of our sojourning. You'll find yourself smiling with understanding as you read about her all-too-familiar experiences living and serving abroad. The prompts at the end of each chapter give space for meaningful reflection and response as Burkholder emphasizes the power of remembering God's faithfulness to us and telling others about it. Every global worker can benefit from adding this book to their library.

—**Heather Fallis**, creator of *Liturgies for a Life Abroad*

This book is a gift for anyone who has ever tried to follow God in unfamiliar places—geographically or spiritually. Through honest, funny, and deeply faithful stories, Eva invites us to remember God's goodness in our own journeys. Her words remind us that we are never alone in the struggle or the laughter, and that every ordinary moment holds a glimpse of grace.

—**Sarah Hilkemann**, Velvet Ashes Director of Operations

As Eva remembers the highs and lows of her own cross-cultural service, she skillfully intertwines the paradox that we can encounter the truth of God's trustworthy character in the midst of each difficulty we experience. Hard and good can both be true at the same time. Her heartfelt liturgies and transparent reflections will assure other workers that they are not alone in the challenges they face. God is present and aware of everything they encounter . . . even if they don't feel it. Whether you have personally served overseas or not, Eva's challenge to remember and tell will inspire you to share your own personal story so that those walking life with you will be encouraged in their faith and join the chorus of praise to worship God and declare his sovereignty and goodness.

—**Lorrie Lindgren**, CEO of Thrive Ministry, *retired*

As a friend, supporter, and occasional participant in a few of the stories contained in this wonderful volume, I'm beyond blessed to see it come into print. Eva Burkholder's life in global work overseas was not glamorous or amazing in the sense we sometimes want our stories of mission to be. It was . . . normal. Slowly, methodically, frustratingly, and painstakingly normal. And that is what makes this book and its stories so encouraging. Eva tells these stories from her decade-plus of answering God's call to a hard place with humor, honesty, and reality that makes these accounts not just true, but lessons in faithfulness for ordinary people—including, but not limited to—those who find themselves serving cross-culturally. Each section's opening prayer resonated with some aspect of my own very different set of life experiences, and they will probably do the same for you. The book's mission is found in her charge to remember and tell. Eva does that and then asks us to do the same. It is a very healthy exercise for all of us, and one that can produce praise, lament, and laughter, sometimes all in the same moment. I commend the book and the process to you.

—**Craig Miller,** Director for Educational Development,
Indigenous Ministries International

Few gifts are as precious as the stories of those who have gone before us. My friend Eva Burkholder has entrusted us with just such a treasure. Drawn by her honesty and vulnerability, I find myself relating to many aspects of this modern-day *Pilgrim's Progress.* It's not just the experiences themselves (some of which my wife and I shared), but Eva's scriptural framing that sets each episode in eternal perspective. *In Every Moment* is an ideal guide for global workers and their teams at any stage of the journey, but also for those who want to prayerfully understand and support the "hard work" of gospel seed sowing (John 4:38).

—**Steve Richardson**, President, Pioneers USA

Eva captures the powerful impact of remembering God's character in her personal and honest stories of pain, confusion, and unbearable strain when she faced the unexpected in her missions journey overseas. *In Every Moment* is about remembering God in our stories. But to remember God's faithfulness is no small task when God appears distant or silent. Eva invites us to remember our stories, to reflect on truth, and even more powerful, she invites us to also press into God's character in life's twists and turns, finding that God is still good. If you want to remember God in your stories, this is a great book to help you on that journey.

—**Elliot D. Stephens**, Global Equip Leader, Pioneers

In this devotional, Eva warmly invites the reader into moments of her ministry life in Indonesia while sharing Biblical truths revealed through these experiences. At the end of each section, she turns the focus toward the reader with scriptures, personal application, and prayers for further reflection.

—**Melissa Wilger**, Albania

This is a must-read devotional designed specifically for global workers! Structured as a 12-week devotional with liturgies, honest Indonesian stories, scripture, and invitations to remember and respond, *In Every Moment* draws you into a simple and beautiful rhythm of reflection. If you're like me, you'll find yourself nodding, "Yes!" and identifying with Eva's stories. But this isn't just about Eva; you're invited to remember your own stories and God's faithfulness to you!

—**Amy Young**, Author, *Looming Transitions,* Founder, Global Trellis

In Every Moment

RECOUNTING GOD'S GOODNESS IN OVERSEAS LIFE

EVA BURKHOLDER

In Every Moment: Recounting God's Goodness in Overseas Life

Pondered Treasures Books
Richardson, TX 57081
www.evaburkholder.com

Paperback ISBN: 978-1-7342190-2-9
Ebook ISBN: 978-1-7342190-3-6
Copy editor: Elizabeth Trotter
Cover design: Thai Martin
Cover watercolor: John-Mark Burkholder
Interior design: Melanie DesPlas
Adelia Font: Carroline Herrera
Author Photo: Ben Cooper
Printed in the United States of America

Dedication

To Mark, my husband, ally, co-laborer, and companion in each of these stories. If you had not been by my side, I might have survived (because Jesus was with me), but it sure would have been a lot harder and a lot less fun.

To my grandchildren. May you hear these stories, as well as the ones your parents tell, and remember the goodness of the Lord. He loves you dearly, and he is worth serving.

To Anna, 1963 – 2000, my beloved teammate, who gave her life to telling others about Jesus. You inspire me.

To Nella, 1968 – 2002, my dear Indonesian friend, who loved any child within her reach and moved mountains to invite them to her Savior. It was my honor to journey with you for a season.

Contents

WEEK FIVE

WEEK SIX

WEEK SEVEN

WEEK EIGHT

WEEK NINE

Preface

The Bible tells us over and over again to "remember" or "do not forget." Only the commands "Do not fear" and "Praise the Lord" appear more frequently. I first explored the concept of remembering while preparing to teach on the life of Mary of Nazareth. When Mary treasured things in her heart, she was remembering. In *Favored Blessed Pierced*, I write:

> In Luke 2:19, treasured (*syntereo*) means "to remember or keep in mind lest it be forgotten." This is the same word that Luke uses in 5:38: "But new wine must be put into new wineskins, and both are *preserved*" (emphasis mine, NKJV).[1]

Mary kept a sort of mental treasure box of "the sayings of the angel, Joseph, shepherds, Elizabeth, Simeon, and even Jesus himself. This way she could remind herself again of the promises, the miracles, the dreams, the amazing visitors, and the fulfilled prophecies."[2] I believe this practice enabled her to remain a faithful disciple even with a heart deeply pierced by pain.

Never have I felt the need to remember God—his character, words, wonders, cross, and resurrection—as much as I have in these troubled and discordant years following the 2020 pandemic. In my turmoil, I found solace in the lament of the psalmist, Asaph:

> I cried out to God for help; I cried out to God to hear me. When I was in distress, I sought the Lord; at night I stretched out untiring hands, and I would not be comforted. . . . "Will the Lord reject forever? Will he never show his favor again? Has his unfailing love vanished forever? Has his promise failed for all time? Has God forgotten to be merciful? Has he in anger withheld his compassion?" (Ps. 77:1–2, 7–9)

But Asaph didn't stop there. He went on:

> I will remember the deeds of the Lord; yes, I will remember your miracles of long ago. I will consider all your works and meditate on all your mighty deeds. (Ps. 77:11–12)

Asaph remembered God's mighty deeds. In doing so, he

answered the questions of his original lament. Of course, his great God who performed miracles long ago had not rejected him. Asaph could certainly trust this holy God who displayed his power and redeemed his people (Ps. 77:13–15). I appreciate the way a pastor friend, Mike Stroh, defines remembering. He says it's "taking something God did in the past, bringing it into the present, and then living in light of it." I think that's what Asaph did.

Seeking to follow his example, I thought about my own life. What have I seen God do that I can choose to remember? When has he shown his power and goodness on my behalf? Immediately I recalled a season when life was hard and, at the same time, God was good.

From 1991–2003, my husband and I served as global workers with a faith-based agency on two tropical islands in Indonesia. I now know that any cross-cultural experience comes with stress, but the last six years of our stint seemed over the top. Break-ins, riots, evacuations, and the deaths of teammates characterized those years.

Fortunately, my mother and mother-in-law kept all the prayer letters my husband and I wrote while we lived overseas, as well as my almost-weekly personal correspondence (at first handwritten snail mail letters, then hard copies of emails). These records, combined with my personal journals, provided rich reminders of God's faithful deeds. In the midst of the struggles, God remembered me, my family, and my teammates and came to our aid.

But remembering for my personal encouragement is not enough. Asaph didn't keep his stories to himself. He boldly spoke out to benefit the next generation:

> We will tell the next generation the praiseworthy deeds of the Lord, his power, and the wonders he has done . . . so the next generation would know them, even the children yet to be born, and they in turn would tell their children. Then they would put their trust in God and would not forget his deeds but would keep his commands. (Ps. 78:4, 6–7)[3]

Like Asaph, I'm telling my stories so my children can know what God did for our family when they were young. I hope this recounting of God's deeds will help them put their trust in him. And I write for my grandchildren. When I look into their bright, inquisitive eyes, I want them to know that God is loving. He is good. He is worth serving. I also write for you, my reader, so your faith might increase and you may be inspired to tell your own stories of God to your descendants.

I shared some of these stories in a photocopied devotional I handed out to family and friends upon our return from Indonesia. Other anecdotes made their way into guest blog pieces, my personal blog, my devotional, *Favored Blessed Pierced,* and in my co-authored workbook, *Grit to Stay Grace to Go.* Now I'm collecting them under one cover as a testimony to God and a document for the next generation.

As I have remembered my years overseas, I am convinced anew that the God who was faithful and good to me in every moment then is still with me now. And he will continue to act according to his character in the days to come.

Introduction

As a seminary student in a school known for its emphasis on the great commission,[4] I frequently heard calls to go as a global messenger to the unreached. The solicitation often sounded something like this:

> WANTED: Men and women to share the hope of Christ with the unreached overseas
>
> QUALIFICATIONS: Love Jesus; adapt to new things, lifestyles, foods; embrace different cultures without judgment; live adventurously
>
> JOB DESCRIPTION: Commit to the goal of evangelism and church planting; complete tasks outside of comfort zone; accept minimal job success; boast few results

When my husband, Mark, and I married, we said "yes" to God's leading. After completing all the necessary steps of joining an agency, training, fundraising, and building a prayer team, we boarded a plane with our ten-month-old son and flew to a country we had never set foot on. (In retrospect we might have benefitted from a survey trip.) We arrived New Year's Eve, 1991.

While I knew our journey would not be easy (I'm a third culture kid from Papua New Guinea, after all), no one could have warned me about what we had truly signed up for. Realities like poor medical care, myriad sicknesses, accidents, deaths, riots, evacuations, danger, loss, steady exit of teammates, and untold amounts of stress.

Looking back, it felt like we focused all our attention and energy on merely surviving from one crisis to the next. Many times, we wondered what we were even doing there and when we should leave. I questioned why I'd dragged my children to such an unsafe place and how I'd lead anyone to Christ.

Despite all that, I (and my family) witnessed the greatness of our God and learned valuable life lessons. I saw the beauty of the body of Christ in action as our team bore each other's burdens. I enjoyed deeper relationships than I ever imagined possible. I experienced answers to prayer, intimacy with God, and personal healing. God manifested his strength amid trauma, producing spiritual growth in myself and others. And in addition, I helped plant seeds of the gospel in a harsh and needy environment.

When I looked only at my circumstances, I was shaken in my spirit, disturbed in my thoughts, and tempted to give up. But I desperately wanted to follow God and find him sufficient for the troubles in my life, so at some point in each crisis, I turned to God's character. His unchanging goodness and love brought me to the only thing necessary—sitting at his feet and listening to him (Luke 10:38–42). Loving him, knowing him intimately, and worshiping him—rather than merely working for him—became my goal.

Some principles I learned on site, at the time of the event. I was young and still had a lot of maturing ahead of me, so other lessons I did not realize until the perspective of time and age helped me to see things more clearly. Now, looking back thirty years later, I know without a doubt that God is mighty and good.

This book is not about a revival or even one church plant. It's not a how-to manual based on miraculous events. This is a recounting of how God revealed himself and transformed me when we stepped out in faith to be a light to the nations. It's a testimony to God.

These stories represent many, many others who serve God faithfully around the world and whose stories will never be told. I tell mine because some of you will relate. I recount them because God uses ordinary people like me to build his church. Each one of us plays a small part in our corner of the world for a tiny slice of history.

For those specifically who serve overseas, I pray that these accounts will help you see that you are not alone. You join a host of others who also grapple with strange illnesses, utter embarrassing language bloopers, navigate house helpers, experience great loss, and doubt their effectiveness. Many others struggle just to make it through the day.

Because I want this book to be more than fun anecdotes of life on a tropical island in a foreign country, I have chosen snippets, both remarkable and routine, that taught a truth about God worth remembering. My desire is that my stories will stimulate you to also remember God's good deeds on your behalf.

Each of the twelve weeks' entries start with a liturgy[5]—a written prayer—introducing the broad topic for that week, followed by six reflections on everyday life. I have composed them in a devotional style so that you can read one a day, then apply a principle, word of encouragement, or challenge to your own situation. Look up the extra Bible verses, answer the suggested questions, and engage the prayers. You can read them in order or skip around, choosing the topics that interest you. Read daily or linger over them as long as you like.

But don't stop there. As you remember your own similar stories, consider what God has taught you, and tell someone else about God's goodness in your life.[6]

Lastly, I acknowledge that there are other people present in these stories—my husband, two sons, and many beloved co-workers—who may have a different perspective than I have relayed here. Where I have mentioned them, they have accepted my words. But what follows is my viewpoint and may not represent theirs. I have also recreated conversations to the best of my recollection and changed some names to protect identities. I also give credit to my husband. He helped co-write our prayer letters in the early days, so his words and ideas are intertwined with mine and used with his permission.

Week One

Liturgy for Partners

Precious Father, thank you for our faithful and caring partners—
friends, family, church members, and interested folk—
who pray for and support us, our agency, and the unreached,
people who work hard, budget every dime, and sacrifice other things so that we can serve you as you've asked us to.

Please remind them how important and vital
they are to us and to all global messengers.
Without them we could not plant your church around the world,
but mostly remind them how dear they are to you.
You see the part they play in serving you,
you see their heart, their needs, and struggles.

In the days ahead, provide for them,
give back abundantly what they give to us.
Only you see what they truly sacrifice,
take care of them, Lord, as you promise to do.
You never let the righteous go begging—
in lean times and in plenty, be with them.

For the challenges that they will face,
prepare and protect them.
Surround them with grace and comfort,
bring friends and physical support,
but mostly show them your character and your presence,
for you alone are with them in every situation.

As they seek to live as ambassadors for you
in their corner of the globe, equip them.
Show them how to represent you
in their homes, churches, workplaces, and communities.

Shine through them so that your light
may penetrate dark places.
May others see their good deeds and glorify you.
May they produce the fruit of light—
goodness, righteousness, and truth—
and find what pleases you.

In the days ahead,
I pray that our partners will walk in the light,
become more and more like you who is true light,
live the way that you enlighten,
and follow the steps you illuminate.

Together with our partners,
I ask that all peoples around the world walking in darkness
will see a great light.
I pray that on those living in the land of deep darkness,
your light will dawn.

Amen.[7]

1

Impossible Request

God Answers Prayer

> *You do not have because you do not ask God. When you ask, you do not receive, because you ask with wrong motives, that you may spend what you get on your pleasures.*
> *James 4:2–3*

We resigned from our jobs and packed up our belongings. The journey to Indonesia had begun. As we pondered all that lay ahead of us, we felt scared, small, and fully aware of our humanity. We realized we had lots of learning and maturing to do. We knew this difficult and frightening venture would stretch us in unexpected ways.

In spite of our inadequacies, we wanted to go wherever God led and do our part in spreading his good news. But we could not do this great work alone. James O. Fraser, serving in China in the early twentieth century, tells his partners:

> God is able to do this and much more, but He will not do it, if we are out here and you at home sit in your easy chairs with your arms folded. Why prayer is so indispensable we cannot just say, but had better recognise the fact even if we cannot explain it.[8] . . . I am not asking you just to give 'help' in prayer as a sort of side-line, but I am trying to roll the main responsibility of this prayer-warfare on you. I want you to take the BURDEN of these people upon your shoulders, I want you to wrestle with God for them.[9]

The task of kingdom-building requires group involvement. We needed our partners to join with us from the get-go, not only after we arrived in Indonesia. But we weren't going anywhere until we had somewhere to stay for a few months while we raised the remainder of our funds and awaited the clearance to get on the plane.

We began praying for inexpensive temporary housing near our sending church where we could maintain some semblance of family life and enjoy some privacy. We shared this need and asked our partners to pray with us. We waited. Some good offers arrived, but we refused them. These places would have been adequate, yet not in line with what we prayed for. We continued to wait and ask. The possible living spaces dwindled.

Confused at God's seeming delay, I examined my heart. I had asked, as the apostle James instructed me to do (James 1:5–8). So had my husband. Our family and partners interceded as well. Perhaps I had wrong motives? Was I selfish to want private space where our baby could sleep well and we could be alone? Was my request too specific, and did I expect too much?

I felt pretty sure that wanting my family to sleep well, have quality time together, and to take care of our son were okay motives. But not if my intention was to escape within the four walls of the house. Our goal was to get to Indonesia, after all. Therefore, we also needed a place where we could fellowship and entertain in order to build relationships and share our vision for our future work.

The very next day after examining my motives, a friend told us of a basement apartment only two miles from my in-laws' home. While attached to a lovely house, it had its own entrance. Even better, it was shrouded in a woodsy area off the main road.

Waiting and trusting required patience, but God answered—abundantly and specifically. Our temporary home became the perfect place to prepare for the start of our new life and to host friends and potential partners. It enabled us to spend precious time with family (even my parents on home assignment visited) before saying goodbye.

Our hosts provided us far more than simply the rooms we lived in. Their generosity allowed us to channel all our funds into getting overseas. And they also became financial and prayer partners, offering this same haven on future home assignments as well.

Even before we left the U.S., God taught me to ask bravely and specifically for what I desired but also to examine my motives so that my requests stayed in line with his will. More importantly, I learned how much we needed our team of prayer warriors. They received the joy of participating in God's abundant provision for us.

God certainly does answer prayer. Sometimes even with bonus points.

Read

Read Psalm 37:4; John 15:7; 1 John 5:14–15.
What do these verses tell you about God?
What do you want to ask the Lord for but are afraid may be impossible, or too much to ask, or more than you deserve?

Recount

Remember (verbally or in writing) a time when God answered a seemingly impossible prayer specifically and even extravagantly. Tell someone about it.

Respond

Lord God, after all these years, prayer still baffles me. But I have learned to confidently ask you for both needs and desires. I have seen you answer "yes," and at other times, "no" or "wait." I have known your generosity and your grace. Thank you that I can ask freely and that, as I seek you, you lead me to desire your will.

2

Rude Awakening

God Doesn't Change

> *Don't be deceived, my dear brothers and sisters. Every good and perfect gift is from above, coming down from the Father of the heavenly lights, who does not change like shifting shadows.*
> *James 1:16–17*

I jolted out of my sound sleep and sat up in the darkness, wide awake. What was that ruckus? *Allahu akbar! Allahu akbar!* (God is great! God is great!) My ears rang. My husband, also awakened beside me, exclaimed in shock, "Whaaat is that?"

His mouth moved, but I could not hear his words. They were drowned out by the call to prayer emanating from multiple loudspeakers on the mosque across the narrow alleyway from our temporary home.

"What time is it?" I screamed to my husband. He fumbled for a watch. It read 4:30 a.m. We laid back down on this first morning of our new life in Indonesia, our hearts pounding. Confused, we heard echoes of the same call, seconds and minutes behind the first from various parts of the city.

This sound was not at all like the church bells that rang in our U.S. hometown—three short peals heard mainly within a few blocks. This deafening sound invaded the depths of my soul. Never had I heard such a din. We had learned that the majority religious group prayed five times a day and that the mosque broadcasted a chanted prayer as a reminder. But never did I imagine that it would start so early, be so loud, or last so long.

When the decibels finally returned to normal fifteen minutes later, I could hear my baby crying. "Poor guy," I muttered as I bounded out of bed to rescue our startled and confused son. "How will we ever get enough sleep? Why didn't someone warn us about this?"

Maybe it was lack of sleep, jet lag, or the myriad cultural changes that had already started to bombard me, but I began to feel miffed. I shared my irritation with the Lord. *Lord, I resent this intrusion of noise into my sleep. A little heads up would have been nice. I thought there was supposed to be a honeymoon period. Did I misread your leading?*

Then snippets of a hymn my mother often sang during difficult times came to mind: "Great is thy faithfulness . . . There is no shadow of turning with thee . . . Thou changest not . . . As thou hast been thou forever wilt be."[10]

Even though I had changed my location, language, home, community, and even my neighborhood noises, there was no shadow or hint of God changing. He stayed the same—faithful as always. His plan for me might involve surprise and unexpected things, but it remained his good and perfect gift. I needed to trust him and not react so negatively after only one day. God did not mislead me; rather, I allowed my expectations to deceive me into thinking I deserved an easier entry into this new place.

With time we did sleep through the call to prayer, but not always. We learned to predict if it would be a couple minutes or last as long as thirty. The regular rhythm of 4:30 a.m., 12:00, 3:00, 6:00, and 7:00 p.m. soon became normal. But we did ask the Lord for a home a little further away from a mosque.

Read

Look up Numbers 23:19; Titus 1:2; Hebrews 6:18; 13:8.
What do these verses tell you about God?
What unexpected event or circumstance requires you to trust in his unchanging character?

Recount

Record a story of when God proved to stay the same even when the outcome or circumstances were different than you expected. Who can you tell?

Respond

Father God, thank you for never changing even when life throws me a curveball. When it feels like I've been misled, remind me that you stay the same and keep your promises. Show me your faithfulness once again.

3

First Days

God Gives Strength to Face New Things

Those who hope in the Lord will renew their strength.
They will soar on wings like eagles; they will run and
not grow weary, they will walk and not be faint.
Isaiah 40:31

During the first weeks in our new home, I updated my mother:

> We started language school this week. Every morning I rise at 6 a.m. and warm my son's bottle in a pot of water on the stove, read a chapter in the Word, and get him up and dressed. Then I tackle the shower. First, I light the instant water heater, then turn the knob to the water, flip the switch for the water pump, and hopefully water will come out of the shower head on the wall. Adjusting the temperature took several days of experimenting. Water runs all over the tile floor, around the toilet, and proceeds to rot the wooden door. Needless to say, the tiles are not in very good condition, and no amount of scrubbing will make them like new again. Nevertheless, I do feel clean and hot water, no matter where it comes from, is refreshing.
>
> Around 7 a.m., our cook arrives to make breakfast. Lest you think this is a great luxury only the rich can afford, let me inform you just how thankful I am for this necessity. Were I to try to concoct something from that region of the house, I would have to rise with the call to prayer! (One weekend I did manage to make grilled cheese sandwiches and tomato soup after lighting the stove about six times, requiring six matches. Cleaning up then took another hour or so.)

We leave our son with the helpers and by 8 a.m., we are seated at our language school for our four hours of study of the Indonesian language. We can walk to school, and we have met many people along the route. The classes are very well structured with practical application in mind. Every morning we learn, practice, and memorize phrases, sounds, grammar, and songs that we can then use in the afternoon when we go out and meet people. Today I wandered around and mostly greeted people and said the few things I can say. Literally: "What name, Mrs.? Mrs. live in where? I originate from USA. Name mine Eva. This child male mine. I in the process of learning Indonesian."

We are in a great neighborhood for learning, and our baby attracts attention. Some of the first questions I learned to answer were his name and age. Mark is more gregarious and just plunges in with words and sign language and manages to communicate. He's learning his way around the city and meets new people every day.

Evenings find us relaxing (exhausted), watching TV (good listening practice), studying, or even writing to you. We are in bed between 9 and 10 p.m. so we're ready to get up and do it all again the next day. As you well know, living in another culture and concentrating on another language is very tiresome.

I think that since we are trying just to get through each day, communicate a little, and learn about this country, we haven't had time to stop and ponder what we have done and whether or not we like it.

In order to face so many new and difficult things, I continually asked God for his help and strength. I clung to his promise that his grace was sufficient for me, that his power works best in weakness (2 Cor. 12:9), that as I put my hope in him, he would renew my strength (Isa. 40:31). Taking the first step out the door required immense effort, opening my mouth another challenge. But I did it. Gradually I learned the language, found my way around the kitchen, and operated the water heater. Life became more manageable.

Read

Meditate on Philippians 4:12–13; Ephesians 3:16; 1 Timothy 1:12; 2 Timothy 4:17.
How has God strengthened you for the new thing you are facing?

Recount

Tell someone how God has given you strength to face something new and difficult.

Respond

Heavenly Father, without your help I would not be able to face new challenges. You give the strength I need to get up each day, study, practice, and learn new skills. Thank you for perfecting your power in my weakness and strengthening me with power through your Spirit. I put my hope in you so that you might renew my strength. Help me to not grow weary as I carry out my responsibilities.

4

Language Bloopers

God Accepts Us Without Fault

> *Therefore, there is now no condemnation*
> *for those who are in Christ Jesus.*
> *Romans 8:1*

Whatever it was, I knew I had been enthusiastically invited to it. As I stood there smiling and nodding, I ascertained the woman was talking about some event that would take place at her house, but all I caught was that it would happen at 2 p.m. on Friday.

At the appointed time I walked up the narrow street to discover what I had been invited to. As I approached the house, I heard music. I did a double take when I saw ladies in formal dress, but it was too late. The host had spotted me and motioned for me to enter.

I followed the other invitees, signed the guestbook, and entered the small home. A man and woman clothed in beautiful traditional garments sat surrounded by older women. Ah ha! Of course, a wedding. I greeted each person, all the while painfully aware that not only was I underdressed in my everyday casual attire, I had brought no gift. Obviously, I was a newbie. My few lessons in Indonesian proved inadequate for even the word "wedding."

Showing up unprepared and inappropriately dressed exposed my introverted dread. Diving in, trying despite failure, overcoming fear of embarrassment, making myself go out and about to try my simple, childlike phrases stretched me. But language and culture acquisition is a slow slog with plenty of laughter, tears, or feeling plain stupid along the way, so I faced my fears and kept going.

After that, I proceeded to learn the language without much mishap until I gained enough fluency and courage to teach Scripture. My teammate offered to mentor me in Bible storying and created an opportunity for me to try out my skills on a new believer eager to learn the Bible. As per my style, I thoroughly prepared the creation story, paying attention to one particular word. We were warned early on to be extremely careful about this word that had tripped up and embarrassed many a global worker. I should have known better.

In Indonesian, many adjectives can be formed from root words by adding the prefix "ke" and the suffix "an." But there is one notable exception to this rule. The adjective "ashamed" cannot be formed this same way because then it means something totally different, something one does not usually say in public. My story proceeded well until I got to the creation of Adam. Instead of explaining that he was naked and unashamed, I said he was naked and had no genitals.

My disciplee's lips curled ever so slightly. Immediately I recognized my *faux pas*, backpedaled, corrected myself, and finished the story. My teammate graciously never teased me. (She was sympathetic because she once told a mother her baby was a pig!) I tried to forget the mistake, embarrassed by my blooper.

However, the apostle James reminded me that God didn't condemn my mistakes nor find fault with me (James 1:5). He did not beat me up over an unintended language blooper. He loved me even when I messed up. I needed to learn to laugh at myself, pick up, and keep going—not hide in shame.

Read

Check out Psalm 103:13–17; Philippians 3:12–14; Hebrews 4:15–16; James 1:5.
What does God say about you and your mistakes according to these verses?

Recount

Recount a time when God reminded you that he accepts you even though you messed up. Make a plan to tell someone about it.

Respond

Lord, thank you for not finding fault with me. Thank you for helping me learn a foreign language and giving me courage to forge ahead even when I make mistakes. Continuing to face my blunders indicates maturity, so help me to persevere in whatever new challenge lies ahead of me.

5

Health Hazards

Jesus is Able to Heal

And the prayer offered in faith will make the sick person well;
the Lord will raise them up.
James 5:15

Living overseas presented a daily hazard to our health. We initially lived in a crowded city reputed to be a hotbed for all kinds of allergies and bugs because of its location and pollution. Almost immediately, our son came down with fevers, diarrhea, and chest and ear infections. My husband had a mystery virus which hung on for three weeks. The doctor tested for typhoid, hepatitis, and malaria—all negative. I had an itchy spot on my leg that I thought was a mosquito bite, but it never went away until I treated it as a fungus (later I realized it was ringworm).

All manner of pests like flu, giardiasis, diarrhea, and "skin funkies" (our term for any kind of unidentified itch or fungal infection) appeared in regular waves. My husband frequently battled intestinal bugs and eventually developed chronic irritable bowel syndrome. Such was the reality of life and comprised a large amount of our time—diagnosing, taking care of, or recovering from illness.

It was difficult enough to be sick myself, but mothering sick children was even harder. Navigating a new medical system in a foreign language hampered my ability to seek care. One week I felt so frustrated and helpless about my ill son that I shed tears every day, begging the Lord to give wisdom and healing. Another time a severe bout of yet another unnamed virus coincided with a round of culture shock and homesickness, making it harder to bear.

From the start, we reached out to our partners committed to pray for us, entreating them to ask God for healing. They graciously obliged. We got better. I reported our recovery in the next correspondence. We immediately got sick. I asked for prayer again. This cycle repeated so often that I stopped sharing requests or praises for healing. And it seemed we got sick less often.

This pattern appeared superstitious, like a formula for illness prevention. And I felt sure that wasn't how Jesus's healing actually worked. In Matthew chapters 8–10 alone, I discovered why I was so tempted to write my own "how to receive healing" list. Such a list includes things like:

- Wrap up my prayers with "if you are willing." (Matt. 8:2)
- Expect immediate results. (8:3, 13; 9:22)
- Apply the secret magic of Jesus's touch. (8:3, 15; 9:25)
- Get others to ask on my behalf. (8:5)
- Don't ask at all, just wait on God. (8:14)
- Rebuke "storms" and demons. (8:26, 32)
- Confess all my sins first. (9:2)
- Follow Jesus radically by giving up home and family. (8:2; 9:9)
- Beg for mercy. (9:27)
- Exercise great faith, believing Jesus has authority. (8:10; 9:22, 28–29)

I was guilty of trying to create a perfect formula for healing. But Jesus didn't prescribe a health elixir. Rather, he offered his power to heal and, more so, his compassion toward those in affliction. He ministered to each person individually in the way he knew they needed. Likewise, he saw our unique situation and heard our prayers.

I realized that I could bring my requests to the Lord, and he would give me what he considered good (Matt. 7:7–11). Jesus was compassionate. He came for the needy. He was willing to heal and answer our prayers. He would perform miracles for us, but they might not look like the ones in the Gospel of Matthew.

Gradually I realized our bodies needed to adjust to the

onslaught of new germs accosting our systems. Our physical healing was not proof of God's love nor the tenacity of my faith. So I kept lifting up my requests and needs. Then I asked God how he wanted to act, how he wanted to heal. I believed he would respond as he saw fit.

Read

Skim Matthew 8–10; James 5:14–16; Hebrews 11:1.
What "formula" might you be tempted to apply to your need for healing?

Recount

Recall a time when God answered a prayer, particularly for healing, but not according to your formula. Who can you tell?

Respond

Jesus, I turn to you, the one with complete authority and deep compassion. I follow you in faith and trust you to heal. Show me when I am counting too much on a human formula or expecting you to heal in a certain way because I have said or done the "right" thing. I keep asking for healing because you have invited me to do so. And I trust that you have heard me and will answer.

6

Avoiding Driving

God Makes Us Competent

Not that we are competent in ourselves to claim anything for ourselves, but our competence comes from God.
2 Corinthians 3:5

Columnist and humorist Erma Bombeck remembers her visit to Indonesia: "Once you see the drivers in Indonesia, you understand why religion plays such an important part in their lives. After a day as a passenger in a car, I would have worshiped the hotel draperies if I had thought they would protect me from bodily harm."[11]

My visiting father-in-law, too, after only five minutes in the car, remarked, "No wonder you guys so often ask for prayer for driving."

I was outright afraid to drive. Operating the car was not the problem since I had experience with manual transmission and driving on the left-hand side of the road as a teenager. The issue was dealing with other drivers and everything else jockeying for position on the crowded streets.

As in other countries, drivers didn't follow traffic rules as strictly as in the West. They ignored lanes, passed whether there was room or not, pulled out in front of other cars without looking, and stopped anytime, anywhere. On top of all this, the roads were clogged, not only with cars, buses, trucks, and scooters, but also with bicycles, pedestrians, pushcarts, horse-drawn carts, beggars, vendors, as well as various dogs, chickens, and water buffalo.

Many streets were no wider than alleys, some more suited to pedestrian traffic. Most roads desperately needed repair. The alleys wound everywhere with no discernable pattern. Drivers failed to heed signs or blinkers or oncoming traffic. Aggression was the rule.

Needless to say, we had to watch constantly and anticipate everything. Driving defensively took on a new meaning. Rude was as rude did, so if I cut someone off or pulled out in front of another driver, no one took notice.

Considering all this, it's no wonder I felt fearful getting into a car, let alone driving it. But not driving at all wasn't practical. David Benner in *Surrender to Love* says,

> Fearful people live within restrictive boundaries. They may appear quite cautious and conservative. Or they may narrow the horizons of their life by avoidance and compulsion. They also tend to be highly vigilant, ever guarding against life's moving out of the bounds within which they feel the most comfortable.[12]

Trying to control my world by not driving backfired. It kept me from independence and hindered my goal of building friendships and participating in community life. My life verse (2 Cor. 3:5) reminded me I wasn't in this alone. My sufficiency, my power, and my competency came from God, not me. Therefore, I could depend on him to give me what I needed to minister in my new context, starting with facing my fear of driving.

Finally one Sunday morning, I could avoid my fear no longer. My husband was sick, and I wanted to attend the service. Mark's illness afforded the ideal opportunity to drive myself and my son to church. I took the plunge. With a constant prayer on my lips, I gripped the steering wheel, carefully turned onto busy streets, made it successfully to the church, and parked the car.

I could do this. It wasn't so bad after all. With relief, I entered the small building, sat Lane on my lap, and sang praises to God for his protection and enabling. What a joy it was to worship with those believers that day. Choosing to depend on the power of God to give me what I needed to tackle my fear brought satisfaction and peace. I even made it back home again.

Read

Peruse Psalm 46; 2 Corinthians 12:9–10; Hebrews 13:5–6.
What do these verses tell you about God?
What might you miss because you are avoiding facing your fear?

Recount

Tell someone about a time when God gave you competence to do a hard thing.

Respond

Abba Father, empower me with your sufficiency to face my fears and not be controlled by them. I praise you and trust that you are powerful enough to walk with me through any difficult situation. Help me stand and face it and take the next step.

Week Two

Liturgy for Cultural Adjustment

Lord God, I'm full of emotions—
I'm excited to be here, delighted I'm still breathing.
I'm proud I've learned my way around the neighborhood
and can speak a few helpful phrases,
that I successfully purchased toilet paper
and navigated bathing with buckets and dippers.
I'm eager to meet more people
like those who have shown me generous hospitality.

But more so, I feel inadequate, insignificant, overwhelmed.
Will I ever master this language or this culture?
I'm perplexed, confused, even terrified
at what I don't understand.
Actually, I'm not sure I understand much of anything.
I feel like a toddler, taking one hesitant step forward
only to fall down abruptly.

Why am I here again? What am I doing?
I confess I'm not as happy as I think I should be.
I came because you led me to this place, Lord.
I left family and friends to follow you.
I wanted to be a disciple that takes
your kingdom to faraway places,
to love those who don't know you love them.

But instead, all I'm doing is failing to sleep well,
repeating my ten simple phrases,
battling illnesses and germs,
keeping ants out of the cereal,
rodents out of the house,
and trying to survive.
In addition to adjusting to new ways to do life,
I'm trying to manage hired help
and maneuver beggars at my gate.

I wonder if I'll ever figure it out,
I wonder if I'll ever fit in or call this place home.
I didn't expect to like everything,
but I thought I'd like something.

I need you, Lord, so desperately.
I don't have any clue what I'm doing, but you do.
You haven't asked for my perfection, only faith.
I trust you with this new life of mine.

I remind myself that you created all peoples
and understand all languages,
that you are King of the nations
and Lord of the harvest.

I know you called me here,
I know you will equip me,
I know that I am not alone,
that you came over the waters with me.
You will go with me and grant me success.

Amen.[13]

7

Rat Extermination

Jesus Has Crucified Our Old Self

> *For we know that our old self was crucified with him so that the body ruled by sin might be done away with, that we should no longer be slaves to sin . . . count yourselves dead to sin but alive to God in Christ Jesus. Therefore do not let sin reign in your mortal body so that you obey its evil desires.*
> *Romans 6:6, 11–12*

We had been warned that the time would come and been told how to do it. Still, my husband proved reluctant to snuff out the life of the critter living in the laundry room, mostly due to the method of execution.

In Indonesia, rats were commonly killed with rat glue. This seemed like no big deal until we realized the glue only performed its intended purpose—to stick two surfaces together. In this case, the rat to the paper. This meant the rodent still breathed even when trapped, and Mark would need to choose a method to do the poor creature in. To further complicate the situation, this was his first experience with a rat. Mice? No problem. Cockroaches? Common stuff. But rats?

After two weeks of stalling, my intrepid spouse finally mustered bravado and decided to give it a go. Not fully understanding the procedure, he asked our helper to set the trap. She spread the glue onto some wadded-up newspaper and placed the bait in the center of the goop.

A few hours later, Mark peeked through the window of the condemned room. It had worked. Stuck in the glue, Mr. Rat wiggled desperately to get out of the mess. For a split second, Mark actually felt sorry for the rat, but before he could change his mind, he rushed in and bashed it over the head with a pipe. There, done.

After surviving this first rat kill, Mark didn't relish the thought of having to repeat the process. But we soon discovered our deceased rat came from a community inhabiting our house. It was not uncommon to be watching a movie at night only to have a rodent scurry along the floor, behind the cabinet, and out into the courtyard.

Mark continued eliminating our rodent colony, imagining himself quite the pest control, until we encountered a particularly pesky one. Every night for several weeks, the sound of feet scurrying around the curtain of our bedroom window awakened us. He put out rat glue with various bait. When that failed, he located rare and more expensive rat traps. Nothing worked. We sought the advice of friends and "experts." All concluded this must be a nesting mother rat. Why else would she ignore the various and sundry treats we had set out for her?

Finally, one night we could take it no longer. When the rat woke us, we jumped out of bed. My husband threw on the light, causing the creature clinging to the curtain to take a flying leap across the room and run for cover behind the wardrobe. Mark grabbed a local broom (a tight bundle of coconut or palm leaf ribs) and slowly pulled the piece of furniture away from the wall. I planted myself at the other end. The critter tried to run in my direction, but I wildly swung another broomstick in its path, so it headed back towards Mark. He jabbed and caught the creature in the fibers of the broom, spearing it like a kabob. Empowered by adrenaline and lack of sleep, Mark thrashed it up and down until it finally lay dead in its own bloody pool. We had waged the battle and won.

Looking back, I'm amazed at how much energy and persistence it took to kill one rat, let alone exterminate them all. Similarly, the apostle Paul instructed us to not let sin reign in our lives or obey its desires (Rom. 6:12). So why don't I tackle my flesh with the same intensity and focus as we did in eliminating our rat infestation?

I have let idolatry, pride, discord, unkind words, and envy creep around the walls of my heart. If I indulge them, they will multiply and govern my life (Rom. 8:5–7). However, since I belong to Jesus, I am a new creation (2 Cor. 5:17). My old self was crucified with him so that I am no longer a slave to sin (Rom. 6:6). He has set me free, and I don't have to gratify those desires (Gal. 5:1, 13–21). Therefore, those fleshly desires are dead to me (Col. 3:5–8 NASB). Instead, I choose to live by the Spirit and follow his leading (Gal. 5:24–25).

Read

Meditate on the verses above along with Romans 13:12–14.
What provision has Christ given you to deal with the "rodents" in your life?

Recount

Recall a time when you overcame an old sin pattern. Who might be encouraged by your example?

Respond

Precious Jesus, you tell me that my old self has been crucified and that I am a new creation. Teach me to live out of my new identity, not gratifying my old desires, but instead walking in your Spirit. Just like we strategized, worked hard, and consistently waged war on the rats in our home, help me to reject my flesh so it will not take over who I truly am.

8

Hard to Love

Jesus Loves Us So We Can Love Others

A new command I give you: Love one another. As I have loved you, so you must love one another. By this everyone will know that you are my disciples, if you love one another.
John 13:34–35

"Will you give me your old shoes? And how about that watch?" he asked my husband. It was the first time Mark had met this young man. "When will you come back with the shoes?" he kept insisting.

As soon as a lady in my neighborhood saw my baby in my arms, she screamed, *"Lucu. Lucu sekali"* (Cute. Very cute). She then pinched his cheeks until they were red and continued to grab at them until he cried. Then she laughed.

When my husband told his tutor that he no longer wanted to continue with music lessons, the man sat in stunned silence. He looked pained as though Mark had personally targeted him. When he caught his breath, he pled with Mark, pressuring him to continue the lessons. Eventually, my husband discovered the tutor had already purchased something and without Mark's ongoing payments, he'd be in debt.

"Do you use birth control? What kind?" my neighbor randomly asked me. "How much money does your husband make?" was yet another common query.

These were just a few of our daily encounters that tempted me to ignore, avoid, and stereotype our new hosts and neighbors. I was supposed to "love the people," but some days loving the local populace was the last thing I wanted to do. How would I answer the next partner or pastor in the U.S. who asked me, "Do you love the people?" Did crossing the sea make it any easier to love them? Would I ever get to a place where their antics and quirks would be less annoying?

As I wrestled with my lack of love, I realized that it was not possible for me to love "the people." The overall people group living their daily lives around me comprised a mass of nameless faces. But I could love individuals whom I came to know personally. Real humans I called by name like Yanti, Mimin, Debi, and Sri. Precious individuals created uniquely by God, not according to a stereotype. They weren't my "target people." They were God's image-bearers to love and serve.

"Oh Jesus," I cried, "I need your love to flow through me to those who constantly ask me for handouts, tell me how to rear my children, invade my personal space, and make my son cry. You love me when I don't deserve it. You set aside your rights and gave your life for me. In the same way, I want to demonstrate your love so that they can see how much you love them."

I sought advice from seasoned workers to understand the appropriate ways to respond to cultural differences and unpleasant behaviors. I prayed for wisdom as I spoke and interacted with my neighbors. Mostly, I asked Jesus for his love to flow through me so that I could love the individuals I met. As I developed relationships, I began to see not their stereotypical negative traits, but rather the gentleness, politeness, and creativity within each beautiful soul.

Read

Meditate on John 15:13; 1 Corinthians 13:6–8; Galatians 5:22; Philippians 2:5–8.
What would it look like to love your neighbors as Jesus loves you?

Recount

Remember a time when God gave you supernatural love for someone who was hard to love. Who can you tell?

Respond

Lord Jesus, I know that I have your Spirit in me. I know that he cultivates love in me. Teach me how to let your love flow through me to people whom I find difficult to love. Give me eyes to see your beautiful image in each one. Show me what it means to love them as you loved me.

9

Outstretched Hands

God Cares for the Poor Through Us

All they asked was that we should continue to remember the poor, the very thing I had been eager to do all along.
Galatians 2:10

There it was again. The rattle of the gate. "Missus! Missus!" an old woman called.

Sigh. Another person asking for money. Just earlier that day, numerous children had surrounded my car almost every time I stopped at a red light on my way to the shops. And then when I entered each store, people with physical handicaps sat directly in the entry way. All these needy persons stretched out their hands expecting, asking, begging for a few coins.

Encountering the poor made me extremely uncomfortable even though I knew Jesus said we would always have them among us (Matt. 26:11). At the time I felt like they targeted me specifically because my skin was white, my hair was fair, and I drove a car.

I struggled to know how to respond. I could simply ignore them, or I could give a pittance every time. I wondered, too, if I put money in an outstretched hand, would it actually help the person that needed it, or would it line the pockets of someone exploiting their youth or handicap?

I decided to discover what God said about the poor. I found these principles in the Old Testament:

- God has a heart for and is concerned about poor and needy persons. (Ps. 9:18; 37:25; 146:7; Isa. 58:6–7)

- Give to poor ones and lack nothing. Conversely, close your eyes to them and be cursed. (Prov. 28:27)
- Don't oppress poor people. Being kind to needy ones honors God. (Prov. 14:31)
- Do not charge interest on your loans or take collateral. (Exod. 22:25–27; Deut. 24:10–13)
- Do not take advantage of a hired worker who is poor. Pay them daily wages. (Deut. 24:14–15)
- Sell food at cost. Hire the poor person rather than take him as a slave. (Lev. 25:35–37)
- Don't be tightfisted. Be open-handed, freely lending what others need. Give generously, without a grudging heart. (Deut. 15:7–11)
- Do not deny justice to the oppressed and the impoverished. (Amos 2:6–7; 5:12)

And these principles from the New Testament:

- Give to the one who asks. (Matt. 5:42)
- God will reward those who give. (Mark 9:41)
- Be merciful just as God is merciful. (Luke 6:36)
- The wealthy should be generous and willing to share. (1 Tim. 6:17–19)
- Showing compassion for a needy person demonstrates love. (1 John 3:17)
- Giving must be done in love and cheerfully. (1 Cor. 13:3; 2 Cor. 9:7)

From my study, I determined that the church should take collections to give to people in need and that I should give both money and material possessions, generously and with right motives. But I also noted that most giving and receiving stays within the context of the body of Christ (Acts 2:42–47; 4:32–37) in response to a famine (Acts 11:27–30; 24:17; Rom. 15:25–29). The apostles (1 Cor. 16:1–4; 2 Cor. 8:17–21) and deacons (Acts 6:1–3) distribute funds, although the exact method and amounts are not mentioned.

Based on these broad principles, I made bags of rice to hand out with a word of blessing to those who came to my gate. For the children, I gave small, pre-packaged food items (something healthier than sweets) instead of coins so they wouldn't feel pressured to take money back to a potential exploiter.

From my current vantage point, however, I think my desire to find a Christian response was more about assuaging my conscience than true compassion. I did not truly see the people who were poor as God's image bearers. Too often I was simply irritated by their presence and their imposition on my comfort. While I tried, I did not fill every outstretched hand and am still growing in compassion and mercy.

Read

Look up some of the verses referenced above.
How does God feel about those in need in your context?
What principles can you apply?

Recount

Revisit an experience when God used you to help someone in need. How can you preserve this story, and who might you share it with?

Respond

Lord, I confess that seeing people begging makes me uncomfortable. I realize I will always be wealthier than someone, so show me how you want me to give out of my abundance in my context.

10

Culture Shock

Jesus Invites Us to Rest

Come to me, all you who are weary and burdened, and I will give you rest. Take my yoke upon you and learn from me, for I am gentle and humble in heart, and you will find rest for your souls. For my yoke is easy and my burden is light.
Matthew 11:28–30

"We are constantly irritated and upset. Our teammates bug us. We don't seem to like anyone or anything," my husband and I complained to a couple on our team.

"How long have you been here?" our new friends asked.

"Six months," we replied.

Their reply came quickly. "Oh, that sounds like culture shock. You need a vacation. It will pass."

They invited us to go with them to the beach. Respecting their experience and advice, we accepted their offer. During the drive to the coast, they told us their own story. Somewhere around the half-year mark, they vented to each other while in the car with their young son. In complete frustration, the husband declared to his wife, "I think I'm about to go off the deep end."

From the back seat came the voice of their son, "Can I come too, Daddy?"

As you can imagine, this broke the tension, bringing laughter and renewed vigor to continue on.

After a lovely vacation, our irritation faded and forbearance returned. Our teammates were correct. We needed some time away. And we learned the importance of taking breaks. Sometimes only a few hours spent at a pool or a restaurant were sufficient. Or a day at the beach. Other times a full-on-get-away-from-it-all-vacation was in order. A little "change of scene and society,"[14] as Elizabeth Bennet describes it in the mini-series, *Pride and Prejudice,* was good for everyone. More importantly, Jesus offered us rest, and we took it.

But I didn't know then what I know now. These days I would be more strategic in determining the kind of rest I needed. In a podcast interview, Dr. Saundra Dalton-Smith says that rest "is not about cessation. It's about refreshing—looking for ways to restore the damage that was done in the working. Rest is for restoration."[15] In her book, *Sacred Rest,* she describes the seven types of rest we need.

During those first months, I probably needed *physical rest* just because daily living required so much energy and because I was also pregnant at the time. Furthermore, the new night noises interrupted my precious sleep—the call to prayer, the truck driver warming his diesel engine, the electricity going off or coming back on, cats mating and raising kittens in the rafters, critters running across the roof, and the night watchmen clanging on the metal pole outside my window to reassure me all is safe. I required naps along with physical exercise.

We were in the throes of language learning, so I needed *mental rest.* Around that time I also assisted a local quilting ministry, creating mock-ups of small projects. I didn't realize it then, but this provided the perfect mental break for me. Sewing and crafting allowed my brain to go into a quiet space and recharge.

Since I struggled just to have a regular quiet time with a toddler running around, language classes, and daily duties, I'm sure I needed *spiritual rest.* A personal retreat or a date with Jesus would have been ideal.

Seeking fellowship with our wiser colleagues provided the *emotional rest* I needed. They let me express my feelings, tensions, and frustrations instead of holding them inside. Crying a lot, both with the Lord and with teammates, also relieved pent-up stress.

I realize now that God gave me life-giving friends. They poured into me, not requiring that I always reciprocate. Gathering together and laughing hysterically provided *social rest.*

I did not have phone or computer screens in my face like I do now, but my senses were overloaded in other ways. I was bombarded with noise—dogs barking and fighting, beggars and salesmen calling, chickens and geese squawking, motorcycles and cars honking. There were few places to go to that were totally quiet. My irritation and agitation indicated my need for *sensory rest.*

And lastly, I needed *creative rest*. Since I spent the first years in a crowded city, my vacation to the beach was on point. Finding a place of beauty to unlock creativity was just what I needed.

Read

Check out Exodus 33:14; Psalm 116:7; Mark 6:31; 1 Corinthians 16:18; Philemon 1:7.
What type of rest do you most need?
What insight do these verses give you about getting that rest?

Recount

Recall a time when God gave you true restorative rest. Who might benefit from hearing about your experience?

Respond

Savior Jesus, thank you for helping me get some rest even when I don't fully understand what I need. Thank you for ultimately being my source of true rest. Help me to discern what my body, soul, spirit, and mind need so that I can find restoration and refreshment that enables me to continue serving you and others.

11

I Hate Ants

God Enables Us to be Diligent

We want each of you to show this same diligence to the very end, so that what you hope for may be fully realized. We do not want you to become lazy, but to imitate those who through faith and patience inherit what has been promised.
Hebrews 6:11–12

I noticed that tell-tale movement in my Tupperware™ container of Honey Stars™ breakfast cereal. *No way!* Those annoying ants had found a way into the canister again! *Of course they went for the sweet food, but how did they penetrate the seal?* I had carried these plastic containers overseas in my luggage because they were considered the tightest and best seals available. But even Tupperware did not stand a chance against Indonesian ants.

Because we lived in a warm climate, geckos, flies, mosquitoes, spiders, and other bugs shared our home. Yes, cockroaches existed too, but if I kept the house clean, they were the least invasive species. Besides, I had learned to battle roaches from my upbringing in Papua New Guinea.

But I hated ants. The variety of them astounded me. Teeny tiny ones, black ones, red ones, large ones, biting ones, wiggly ones. Scouts on the prowl for food searched for the slightest hint of neglect on my part, a crumb on the floor, or a poorly washed peanut butter knife. Almost daily, I found a trail of ants somewhere in the house.

But keeping a clean space did not deter them either. Finding no easy pickings, they attacked our stored food, often our preciously guarded imported items. And when the insects did manage to infiltrate a box of crackers or a container of brown sugar, I had double the work to get rid of them. I could not just throw the contents away, especially if they were prized or expensive food items. My biggest peeve was that no matter what I did, ants could not be eradicated permanently. They always returned.

In my battle with the ants, some days I won. Other days they prevailed. I tried everything to keep them at bay. I purchased ant baits to put beside the trail. Hopefully, they would eat the poison and take it back to their nest to kill the colony. I transferred all dry goods into containers, making sure to carefully seal every lid every time. I then set the containers on a free-standing shelf, taking care that nothing touched the walls around it so the ants could not access the food items via the wall. Then I went further and placed each foot of the shelf in a plastic lid dusted with boric acid so they would not climb up the shelf legs.

But all of this was merely a temporary solution. If I didn't carefully seal a lid, if a chip bag slipped back against the wall, if the boric acid ran low, or if the baits hit their expiration date, the ants charged in. Since I could not beat them, how might I join them? According to Proverbs, I could learn something from ants:

> Go to the ant, you sluggard; consider its ways and be wise! It has no commander, no overseer or ruler, yet it stores its provisions in summer and gathers its food at harvest. (Prov. 6:6–8)

> Ants are creatures of little strength, yet they store up their food in the summer. (Prov. 30:25)

I certainly could not be a sluggard where ants were concerned. Any slacking in my strategy or daily attention would result in an infestation. This daily vigilance reminded me to face other challenges in my life with the same zeal.

I could be wise and resourceful. I could store up provisions, plan ahead, and be prepared for hard times. This meant more than just financially, but also emotionally. Building up my energy would give me reserve for the traumatic and tough times ahead.

I could lean on my community. As ants needed a colony to survive, I needed others to help me achieve my goals. I needed my team. I could not walk my journey alone. Some of my team might forge ahead to scout out possibilities, but when it came to harvest, it took the whole group.

I could also be hard working, diligent, and persistent. Like the ants, I felt tiny and weak, but I could not give up. Instead, I would do my part in building God's kingdom.

Read

Open your Bible to Proverbs 31:25–31; 1 Timothy 4:14–16.
In what way can you be more like the persistent insects you battle regularly in your corner of the world?

Recount

Recall a time when God enabled you to be resourceful and diligent although you lacked strength and size. Who can you tell?

Respond

Father God, just as I was diligent and persistent in keeping ants out of my house, I need you to help me be just as diligent in my work and service of you. Thank you for my friends, family, small group, and others around me who help me persevere.

12

House Help

God is Our True Helper

But as for me, I am poor and needy; come quickly to me, O God.
You are my help and my deliverer; LORD, *do not delay.*
Psalm 70:5

As we prepared for home assignment, our house helper, Sue, asked me, "Who is your helper in America?"

"Oh, I don't have one," I replied.

"*Kasihan* (pity)," she responded.

I launched into an explanation of automatic dishwashers, large capacity washing machines, clothes dryers, vacuum cleaners, running hot water, and well-sealed houses to deter dust accumulation. Where we lived, she and I had none of those amenities.

Instead, it was common, expected, and, one could argue, even necessary to hire a *pembantu* (literally "one who helps"). Since managing a home required much more effort than it did in the West and because I also wanted to participate in ministry, having some help was, well, helpful.

Open doors and windows in that warm climate meant that our house accumulated dust and dirt readily. Horse-drawn carts traversing the streets outside necessitated daily sweeping and mopping of the floors. The bathrooms also required daily cleaning to prevent mold growth in the floor-to-ceiling tiled space. Small washing machines meant multiple loads a day (especially with cloth diapers) and each item hung out to dry. Fresh produce was first purchased in an open-air market and then sanitized. Almost everything was cooked from scratch, and dishes were washed by hand in boiling water heated on the stove.

In the absence of handy grandparents, a helper provided babysitting while I attended language classes.

Though I desperately needed assistance as I adjusted to life in a foreign context, at times it felt more like an intrusion than a luxury. I struggled with having another person in my space and taking some of the roles that identified me as a wife and mother. I enjoyed doing many household tasks and wanted to ensure I could maintain our family routine and rear our sons.

For me, finding the right helper made all the difference. My first one, whom I liked a lot, quit after only a few weeks. Since I was so new to the culture and language, I never really understood why she left. My second helper, although kind and caring to our babies, recorded higher prices on her written market receipts and pocketed the difference.

By the time I hired my third helper, Sue, I had ascertained what worked best for me and our family. Sue started after breakfast and worked only half a day, so that I could feel like I had my home to myself most of the day. She did the tasks that I preferred not to do and babysat for short periods when I ran errands or swam laps during the boys' rest time.

Sue's assistance freed me up to homeschool my sons, write a Sunday School curriculum, lead Bible studies, and visit the women I mentored. Furthermore, I fulfilled the cultural expectation of boosting the economy and providing a livelihood for a local woman by sharing from my wealth. Sue was also a source for language practice and my most natural avenue for sharing the gospel.[16]

While Sue made my daily life more manageable, she also served as a tangible reminder of my true helper. The Hebrew word for "helper" in Scripture—*ezer*—appears twenty-one times in the Old Testament. Of those references, two refer to the woman God created. God calls her "a suitable helper"—*ezer kenegdo*—to the man (Gen. 2:18, 20). Three others refer to military aid (Isa. 30:5; Ezek. 12:14; Dan. 11:34). And the remaining sixteen refer to God as the helper of his people. For example:

> There is no one like the God of Jeshurun, who rides across the heavens to help you and on the clouds in his majesty. . . He is your shield and helper and your glorious sword. (Deut. 33:26, 29)

> I lift up my eyes to the mountains—where does my help come from? My help comes from the Lord, the maker of heaven and earth. (Ps. 121:1–2)

From these references, I concluded that an *ezer* is a strong helper, an ally, one who comes to the aid of another, often in times of battle. While Sue relieved my household burdens, God relieved my spiritual and emotional burdens. He came quickly to my aid (Ps. 70:5). Whenever I called and lifted my eyes to him, he was there. Just like he promised.

Read

Peruse Psalm 20:2; 33:20; 115:9–11; 124:8; 146:5.
What do these verses tell you about how God is your helper?
What help from him do you need at this time?

Recount

Who might benefit from hearing about a time when God helped you in ways no one else could?

Respond

Lord God, you are my ezer, my helper, who rushes to my aid in times of need. I am so grateful I benefitted from help in the home when living overseas. But ultimately, you are the one who helped me most, by being with me in every circumstance, every trial, every time I felt inadequate and alone.

Week Three

Liturgy for Spiritual Armor

Lord, today I put on my armor.
I take my stand against the devil's schemes.
I acknowledge that my real struggle is not against other humans
but against the spiritual forces of evil.
Therefore, I protect and arm myself so I can stand my ground.

I put on the belt of truth
so that the enemy cannot attack the veracity of your Word
and make me doubt you, your attributes, and your promises.

I put on the breastplate of righteousness
so that the enemy cannot lead me to sin
or condemn me of sins you died for
because Jesus's blood has made me holy.

I put on the shoes of the gospel of peace
so that the enemy cannot bring disharmony
or enmity between me and others
or between me and you because we are all unified in Christ.

I take up the shield of faith
so that I can extinguish the lies and accusations of the enemy
by believing you are who you say you are
and will do what you say you will do.

I take up the helmet of salvation
so that the enemy cannot cause me to doubt that I am saved
or try to move me from confidence in my position in Christ.

I take up the sword of the Spirit
so that I can fight the enemy by quoting individual verses
which the Spirit brings to mind in time of need.

I pray in the Spirit at all times
with all kinds of prayers and requests.
I am alert and continuously pray for all believers
that together we will fearlessly advance on enemy territory,
declaring the good news so that you might release captives
and build your kingdom.

Lord, I will listen to what you say about
my current struggle or stronghold
rather than following my own feelings or reasonings.
I will act rightly so that the enemy
has no point of attack or accusation.
I will seek to live in unity with you and all those around me.
I will extinguish Satan's lies by believing you.

I realize that because I am your child, the enemy cannot crush me,
touch me, or do anything to me without your permission.
I will counter him with the truth and promises of Scripture.
I ask now for my marching orders and battle plans.
In your name, I stand firm.

Amen.[17]

13

Break-In

God Writes a Unique Story for Us

> *When Peter saw him [John], he asked, "Lord, what about him?" Jesus answered, "If I want him to remain alive until I return, what is that to you? You must follow me."*
> *John 21:21–22*

I awoke, startled. The phone rang persistently. Not the modern kind you can put on silent or send to voicemail. This was an old-fashioned object that sat on a table plugged into the wall in another room. The red letters of the digital clock beside my bed read 4:00.

I threw off my sheet, wondering who it could possibly be. As I lifted the receiver to my ear, my teammate, Joan, cried frantically, "Dan's been cut. Send Mark over here right away."

My unsuspecting husband raced over to their house and discovered quickly that he was not suited to be a first responder. He walked into a scene that will remain engraved in his mind forever. Dan, his good friend and teammate, lay in a pool of liquid on the living room floor with blood splatters on every wall. Joan, a nurse, held their yellow sofa pillows on the wounds. Mark stood still, immobilized by the sight.

"Mark! Look at me, look at me!" Dan's wife's voice brought him back to the present. "Call the police. I cannot remember the number." In a daze he obeyed her bidding. In between soaking up blood and putting pressure on wounds, Joan recounted what had happened.

She heard her bedroom door creak in the early hours of the morning and woke up. Thinking it was one of her children or one of the two friends who were sleeping over, she got up to check. Immediately upon entering the adjacent room, one of three robbers grabbed her and held a knife to her throat. She pushed away the arm holding the knife and screamed.

Her cries aroused her husband who then realized the figures in the doorway were adults, not children. Dan bounded out of the bedroom, saw his wife in danger, and began to fight with the men. In a matter of seconds, he was covered all over with surface cuts and three serious knife wounds—one between the heart and spleen, another deep into his lower back (thankfully missing vital organs), and a third which punctured his lung.

Soon other teammates arrived and transported Dan to the local hospital. Our team, plus a few other expatriate doctors in town, dropped everything to care for him, his wife, and their children. They called the insurance company, arranged a medical evacuation, filled out and signed numerous forms, and stood in line to get exit permits stamped in passports. Teammates took turns sitting with Dan and Joan at the hospital or babysitting children on the team.

I assisted from the background, fielding phone calls and praying. At one point Joan came over to my home with the children for a brief respite. Finally, about twelve hours after the incident, Dan was flown by air ambulance to Singapore for treatment. His family followed on a commercial flight.

This was the first time I had been a part of a tragedy of this magnitude, even if indirectly. My reactions to this crisis surprised me. I wondered why I had been spared. Why was my friend's husband stabbed and not mine? Why had I not seen the blood and felt the horror? I felt guilty for not doing more and just wanted to get back to "normal."

As I meditated on this, the example of the apostle Peter came to mind. When Jesus tenderly commissioned the disciple for his future, Peter wanted to know about his fellow disciple, John.

> "Lord, what about him [John]?" Jesus answered, "If I want him to remain alive until I return, what is that to you? You must follow me" (John 21:21–22).

This same idea is echoed in the words of Aslan to Shasta in *The Horse and His Boy* by C. S. Lewis: "I am telling you your story, not hers. I tell no one any story but his own."[18]

That day, my personal story did not include being a victim of assault. Instead, the Lord God used different means to write my unique story. My job was to follow Jesus where he led me, not to compare my life and my struggles with others.

Read

Read John 21:15–25; 2 Corinthians 10:12–18.
What is God saying to you about your story through these verses?

Recount

Recall a time when God's story for you looked very different from someone else's. Who can you tell?

Respond

Lord, when tragedy and crisis hit us, we react automatically and sometimes don't recognize ourselves. We wonder why we experience some things and others do not. Help me not to compare my situation with others, but to faithfully follow you. I trust you to tell me my story as we write it together.

14

The Aftermath

God Delivers Us from All Our Fears

> *I sought the Lord, and he answered me;*
> *he delivered me from all my fears.*
> *Psalm 34:4*

Our teammate, Dan, underwent surgery to repair the puncture to his lung. He needed time to recover, but he would be okay. Our team was in shock and scared. Excerpts from my letters in the days following the break-in describe my random thoughts:

> On the same night of the attack, we heard of two other believers around town who were awake much of the night, fearful of break-ins. Lots of attempts have been reported and several by expats. As you can imagine, everyone is quite upset. Anyway, we feel attacked spiritually, and so we have asked for renewed prayer for us all.
>
> Another home was broken into and some clothes stolen by reaching in a window. We knew robberies were common, and small things like car stereos and things left in the yard have been stolen. But this is the first time we've experienced an attack on someone personally. The bottom line is that we have always assumed that we were quite safe here. Suddenly, now we know that we are in potential physical danger.
>
> We will take what precautions are necessary. All our windows already have bars, but some don't latch anymore, so we will fix them. We have beefed up the security in our home with motion alarms, dead-bolted doors, and extra lights. And we pray for God's protection.

I have been able to sleep okay until last night [exactly a week after the attack]. The alarm chimed for some unknown reason. After that, I was jittery. One son cried out too, and the other was awake, so I sat up for a while, praying and quoting Scripture verses and songs. I know in my heart that we are relatively safe. Our house is small, and we should hear any attempt to break in. But I wonder who is next? And I know that the Lord's protection doesn't mean we will never experience harm. But my faith is tempted to waiver, thinking that God wasn't quite protective enough in Dan's case. I know that's wrong. This was not a mistake. He is still in control.

I don't see how we would be any safer anywhere else. We have to believe God has a purpose, he knows what he's doing, and he protects us even during traumatic experiences.

The Scripture translation project for a neighboring island was on the verge of starting, and lay training classes were scheduled to begin this week. These have been postponed. So we don't know what the enemy is trying to prevent, but we want to be wise, yet not defeated.

Mark had a trip to the nearby island planned which has also been postponed for a week. None of us feel good about being left by our spouses at this point. Mark and I are doing fine, although I still wonder how it will be here alone at night without him.

Psalm 34 and 37 have been a real comfort to me as well as several verses: "God has not given us a spirit of fear" (2 Tim. 1:7 NKJV). And "Fear not those who harm the body" (Matt. 10:28). God is good, and we do feel him near to us at this time.

Read

Look over Psalm 34 or 37.
What do these verses tell you about God's protection in relation to your fear?

Recount

Tell a friend about a time when God helped you overcome your fear of the actions of evil people.

Respond

Mighty God, help me not to worry about evil people and their wicked schemes, for they will fade away. I commit everything to you. I trust you and take shelter in you. Help me be still in your presence and wait for you to act. Take care of me and my loved ones, Lord. Be our stronghold in times of trouble. Help us and deliver us from the wicked (Ps. 37).

15

Breakdown

God Turns Fear to Gratefulness

Then they cried to the Lord in their trouble, and he saved them from their distress. He sent out his word and healed them; he rescued them from the grave. Let them give thanks to the Lord for his unfailing love and his wonderful deeds for mankind.
Psalm 107:19–21

In the days following Dan's attack, it became apparent that our team leader, Mike, who had carried the brunt of the responsibility, wasn't doing well. As the week wore on, his anxiety ramped up. A week later, he collapsed in a corner of a teammate's home, begging to be put on an airplane to return to the U.S. We called our agency for help, and a counselor arrived—primarily to help Mike, but also to provide counsel for the rest of us.

Mike tells his own story in *Spiritual Survival Handbook for Cross-Cultural Workers* by Dr. Robert S. Miller:

> *What's wrong with me?* I wondered. After seven years of leading a team in Asia, my polished image as a good team leader was showing some serious wear-and-tear around the edges. I fought hard to maintain my reputation, openly criticizing others' strategies and feeling superior in my theological views. Outwardly, I endeared myself to national leaders; inwardly I had come to despise them. And then the storm began. A national leader, once my student and close friend, slandered my good name. Two promising visa plans fell through. Subtle unnamed fears began to keep me awake at night. One of my team members was stabbed: *I can't let*

> *him die on my watch.* The next day, my house was broken into when my son was home alone: *I have to guarantee his safety.* When this final crisis came, I couldn't face it. My world caved in around me.[19]

A month later, the pastor of Mike's sending church came to assist and encourage. His pastor listened patiently as Mike relayed all the struggles, fears, trials, and crises of the past month. Finally, when he could interject, he asked gently, "I've heard about all that you have endured. Now can you tell me how you have seen God work in the past weeks? What are you grateful for?"

Mike sat in silence, unable to respond.

Then his wife spoke up. "I can answer that. I have seen God's protection and care in so many ways. It was a miracle Dan was not more seriously wounded and could survive the twelve hours before the medical evacuation. There were two expat doctors in town who came immediately to help. He did not die. He got out in time. Miraculously, Dan's wounds, though serious, were not life-threatening. Their phone line wasn't cut, and help arrived quickly. The attempted break-in of our home did not succeed. Our son was protected. We stayed in a hotel for rest and safety. A counselor came to help us. You came to visit us."

As Mike listened to his wife's statements of gratitude and praise, his mind woke up. It was as if he could see for the first time through the fog of fear. God had been at work, hadn't he?

Mike turned a corner that day. Of course, everything wasn't immediately better. But witnessing the power of gratitude and praise break the power of fear impressed me greatly. It made vivid and practical what the apostle Paul said: "Do not be anxious about anything, but in every situation, by prayer and petition, *with thanksgiving,* present your requests to God. And the peace of God, which transcends all understanding, will guard your hearts and minds in Christ Jesus" (Phil. 4:6–7, emphasis mine).

Read

Meditate on Psalm 107; Philippians 4:6–7.
What fear is keeping your eyes blind to the hand of God?
What can you give thanks for?

Recount

Think of a time when gratitude helped you turn fear into gratefulness. Who can you tell?

Respond

Lord in heaven, I confess that I often underestimate the power of gratitude in my life. Teach me to look for ways that you are at work, even in the trials and crises.

16

Post-Crisis Care

God Uses the Body of Christ

If one part suffers, every part suffers with it.
1 Corinthians 12:26

While Dan and his family recuperated, we focused inward. Since this was our team's first major crisis, we muddled through. Again, my letters describe it best:

> While things have settled down, the past week has been emotionally draining. We have had to give so much to our team leader and his family that only since the counselors arrived have we been able to process things ourselves and begin to move on. We are sad that we may have to say goodbye to Dan and Joan, and we have many changes ahead since our team leader is also going through such pain.
>
> These past weeks have taught me so much. While it has been a blessing to see love, support, prayer, crying, and hurting in action, I am activity-oriented, and I've gotten my fill of touchy-feely stuff. The judgmental part of me wants to tell people to buck up and go on. However, I am learning to show more empathy, and I realize not all are ready to hear that we have to move on. I'm learning to be more sensitive and caring and giving more. It is draining and hard work, but I want to be teachable.
>
> Although this has been a tragedy, we have already seen the Lord do some great things, one of which is drawing us together as a team and seeing a wonderful display of how the body of Christ kicks in and helps those members who

> are hurting. We still have many hours ahead of sharing and praying together, supporting, and helping each other go on, but God is good and we look forward to what he is going to do. Already we have seen some answers to prayer, and I am praying for other sweet things to come out of this bitter experience.
>
> We feel God near us at this time. We've also felt so much care from friends, our agency, from workers in other towns, and our supporting churches. An event like this could easily be used as the excuse for our team leader to hang it all up and go. Then Mark and I would be tempted to feel abandoned. Of course, I must take every thought captive and not speculate constantly about what may or may not happen.
>
> We must enjoy today and focus on the task at hand. Right now our task is recovery, ministry, and being the body to hurting members. We are trying to take one day at a time, to minister to those who need it, to dwell on the Word, and to pray for one another. My ongoing prayer is that this will be used to draw us even closer together.

A few months later, Dan and his family returned to the U.S. for care and healing and then remained there. Six months later our team leader and his family returned to the U.S. when their visa was not extended. Another couple left when news arrived of a mother's death. A year and a half after we had formed our team, only one other couple besides us remained. Even though the tragedy contributed to our teammates leaving the country, the beautiful outcome was the body of Christ ministering to each other.

Read

Check out Ephesian 4:1–16; Colossians 3:12–17.
How have you seen the body of Christ minister to each other as described in these verses?

Recount

Tell someone about when you experienced the body of Christ functioning fully and beautifully.

Respond

Precious Savior, thank you for giving us the gift of experiencing the body of Christ in action. Keep teaching me to care for and empathize with my brothers and sisters in pain and suffering. Help me to give through my time, prayers, and listening ear.

17

Spiritual Battle

God Gives Us His Power

I want to know Christ—yes, to know the power of his resurrection and participation in his sufferings, becoming like him in his death.
Philippians 3:10

My colleague, Anna, called me. "Would you please come with me to pray for Hilda, one of the local Bible translators? She has been blacking out and speaking in a man's voice."

Feeling a bit terrified and wanting additional backup, I suggested we invite Nella, my local co-worker and mentee, to join us. Together we headed over to Hilda's home.

For two hours, we heard her story, asked questions, read Scripture, and prayed with her. We surmised that someone had put a curse on her. Or perhaps this was a spiritual attack on the lowly translator to thwart the translation work. Hilda seemed to possess an immature understanding of God's power to refute the enemy's attacks. Whatever the case, Satan appeared to prevail at that moment.

We reminded Hilda that God is great and "mighty in power" (Ps. 147:5). In fact, he is "exalted in his power" (Job 36:22). We showed her the apostle Paul's description of power:

> That power is the same as the mighty strength he exerted when he raised Christ from the dead and seated him at his right hand in the heavenly realms, far above all rule and authority, power and dominion, and every name that is invoked, not only in the present age but also in the one to come. (Eph. 1:19–21)

Hilda had already experienced this miracle when she believed the gospel because it is "the power of God that brings salvation to everyone who believes" (Rom. 1:16). Power had been given to her "when the Holy Spirit [came on her]" (Acts 1:8). We asked her to repeat the truth that "the message of the cross is the power of God to those who are being saved" (1 Cor. 1:18).

Next, we reiterated her position in Christ. As a child of God, she has overcome "because the one who is in you is greater than the one who is in the world" (1 John 4:4). We spoke the truth that "there is a greater power with us" (2 Chron. 32:7).

We reminded her that "the Spirit God gave us does not make us timid, but gives us power, love and self-discipline" (2 Tim. 1:7). And yet we unexpectedly acquire God's incredible strength ultimately through weakness (2 Cor. 12:9). We certainly understood weakness.

Finally, we prayed for Hilda that she would know "his incomparably great power" (Eph. 1:18–19) that was also her rightful possession as his daughter.

We left Hilda, knowing she was at peace. We gave her further scripture to study, and Anna promised to check on her progress. She needed to learn she had the ability to keep the enemy away because she was a child of God. Ultimately, we wanted her to hunger for God himself and let his Word penetrate deeply as she translated passages every day.

Hilda persevered. A copy of the New Testament that she helped produce now stands on a shelf in the Museum of the Bible in Washington, D.C., a testimony to the mighty work of God demonstrated through her, Anna, and other faithful translators.

I still don't fully understand the intricacies of God's power, but I want to appropriate it so that I can do good (Acts 10:38), serve others (2 Cor. 13:4), endure in ministry, and overcome the devil's attempts to discourage me (Col. 1:11). I want to tap into his incomparably great power to advance his kingdom.

Read

Look up the verses referenced and meditate on them.
In what areas of your life do you need to appropriate the power that raised Christ from the dead?

Recount

Look back on an instance when God gave you his power to overcome the forces of evil. Who can you tell?

Respond

Help me, Almighty Lord, to understand the incredible greatness of your power for me—the same mighty power that raised Christ from the dead and seated him at your right hand—if I only believe. May the God of hope fill me with all joy and peace as I trust in him, so that I may overflow with hope by the power of the Holy Spirit (Rom. 15:13).

18

Praying God's Word

God Gives Us an Arsenal

Take . . . the sword of the Spirit, which is the word of God. And pray in the Spirit on all occasions with all kinds of prayers and requests. With this in mind, be alert and always keep on praying for all the saints.
Ephesian 6:17–18

"Have you heard of Beth Moore?" a member of a supporting church asked. "She's just written her very first Bible study, and I want to give it to you and your team."

What a wonderful gift from a church. She graciously purchased enough workbooks and the sermon cassettes for our team. This study provided a venue for my teammates and me to fellowship together. As the kind donor predicted, this method of digging into God's Word contributed immensely to our encouragement and growth.

In her study, *Breaking Free,* Moore introduces the practice of praying God's Word. She teaches that I have two weapons—Scripture and prayer. They are doubly potent when employed together.

The apostle Paul, in Ephesians 6:17, used the Greek word *rhema* (utterances) when he referred to the Bible rather than *logos,* the more common term for the entire Scriptures and for Jesus. This inferred using individual verses, or specific words of God, and not just the whole Bible in general.

My former pastor, Tom Koch, described the Bible as being an arsenal of many swords (pulling from Paul's description, *the sword of the Spirit).* As believers, we take out the specific sword we need for the appropriate situation.

I decided to give it a try. I first took notice of the need, burden, or temptation that threatened to strangle me. Then I searched, via a concordance, for verses addressing that concern. For example, when I felt rejected, I found references to God's faithful love and acceptance.

> Can a mother forget the baby at her breast and have no compassion on the child she has borne? Though she may forget, I will not forget you! See, I have engraved you on the palms of my hands; your walls are ever before me. (Isa. 49:15–16)

Then I rewrote these verses switching the pronouns, like this:

> You tell me, Lord, that you will not forget me, even as a mother cannot forget the baby at her breast and has compassion on the child she has borne. You have engraved me on the palms of your hands. Remind me often of your love. (Isa. 49:15–16)

I prayed these verses until they saturated my mind. Over time, the sense of rejection lessened, but I returned to my arsenal of verses whenever I felt that way again.

I then expanded on the practice and wrote prayers for my family and for our work.

For my sons:

> Lord, my prayer is not that you take them out of this world, but that you protect them from the evil one. (John 17:15)

For my spouse:

> Lord, I pray that my husband won't copy the behavior of this world, but he'll let you transform him into a new person by changing the way he thinks. Help him take every wrong and false thought captive and give it to you so you can replace it with truth. (Rom. 12:1; 2 Cor. 10:5)

For the work:

> Lord, I pray that the gospel will come to this island with power, with the Holy Spirit and with deep conviction, not simply with words. (1 Thess. 1:5)

Pages and pages in my journal contained verses written into prayers for my family and the ministry. Praying God's Word became a vital discipline in my journey of faith. This practice helped me pray more consistently and confidently while also leading me deep into the Scriptures. It caused me to meditate on God's promises, and I found encouragement for daily life.

As with all spiritual practices, this form of praying is not a formula or a quick fix to get what I want or to manipulate God into answering my prayers. Instead, I saturate myself in God's own words and state his truth when praying Scripture. I am assured of God's will when I pray his very words (taking care not to take a verse out of context or claim a promise specifically meant for another audience). As a result, I can rest and know that I will receive what I ask for (1 John 5:14–15).

Read

Choose some of your favorite verses and write them into prayers. How might praying the words of Scripture help you overcome threats to your well-being?

Recount

Remember and tell someone about a time when praying God's Word enabled you to overcome.

Respond

Living Word, I take up your Word and pray in the Spirit on all occasions with all kinds of prayers and requests. But my desire is not for spiritual formulas or hacks. No, the one thing I ask, Lord, my one desire, is to dwell in your house all the days of my life, to gaze on your beauty and to seek you in your temple (Ps. 27:4).

Week Four

Liturgy for Times of Brokenness

Lord God who sees, hears, and knows me,
living and serving overseas is breaking me, wrecking me;
highlighting my weaknesses, bringing my faults to the fore,
testing my resilience and patience.
Why does this place seem to make everything worse?

Outside forces weigh heavily—
repeatedly waiting on visa approvals,
traveling in and out of country,
living far away from loved ones and grandparents,
never knowing if our future is secure or safe.
Accidents, emergencies, riots, evacuation,
loss and deaths of teammates and friends,
trauma, sickness, transition, setbacks.

I'm not handling these stressors well, Lord.
I'm afraid I'll collapse under the weight of them.
Furthermore, they shine a spotlight on what's internal—
marital tension, parenting struggles, loss,
anxiety, complaining, negativity, judging, envy,
and pride—always self-righteousness and pride.

I recognize my weaknesses, my inadequacy to endure,
I confess my sin, my arrogance.
I judged others for their faults and their excuses,
I thought my way was the right and best way,
I believed God was fortunate to have me—
until I came here.

Precious Savior, create a clean heart in me
and renew a right spirit within me.
You don't condemn or reject me; you forgive me.
You are close to the brokenhearted,
you invite weary ones to find rest.
You love me lavishly and grow your Spirit's fruit in me,
you promise to complete your good work within me
while preparing good works for me to do.

I realize this journey is more about what you are doing in me:
teaching me to love and know you more;
increasing my faith and decreasing my self-dependence;
growing the Spirit's fruit in me via grieving, mourning,
releasing, saying goodbye, giving up my rights, not judging;
enlarging my circle of friends
and the interdependence of the Body—

than what I am doing for you:
following your invitation into your kingdom-building venture.

If I can love you more, know you more, be more like you,
then it is all worth it.
You, Lord, are worth it.

Amen.[20]

19

Quick to Judge

God Uses Broken People

I thank Christ Jesus our Lord, who has given me strength, that he considered me trustworthy, appointing me to his service. Even though I was once a blasphemer and a persecutor and a violent man, I was shown mercy because I acted in ignorance and unbelief. The grace of our Lord was poured out on me abundantly, along with the faith and love that are in Christ Jesus.
1 Timothy 1:12–14

Early on, I came face to face with my pride. And it was ugly. When the ladies on my team studied the topic of self-significance in our Bible study time, I expressed my desire that our meetings be God-centered, not self-focused. Boy, was I self-righteous!

As I got acquainted with my new colleagues, I heard stories of childhood trauma, abuse, divorce, moral failure, and young faith. This group of women (and men) did not fit my grid of the kind of people I thought God called to his service. I expected God to select the best of the best for leadership, and these folks were subpar according to my high standards.

And yet I knew this authentic and kind group of passionate Jesus-followers had chosen to forsake their comfortable lifestyles to build God's kingdom in a difficult place. I witnessed their submission to God's transforming work in their lives. I rejoiced in the results of their zeal. I had much to learn from them, especially regarding how quickly I judged others.

I didn't know at the time that I was experiencing cognitive

dissonance—a disparity between my belief system and the reality of whom God chooses. My friends' messy lives didn't line up with my beliefs. Obviously, my vetting grid needed to change because it was based on pride.

The Holy Spirit revealed that although I believed his grace saved sinners, in practice, I still held their faults (and even what wasn't their fault) against them. I unconsciously thought their scars negatively impacted their effectiveness. I considered myself more worthy of serving God because I grew up as a TCK (third culture kid) in a family dedicated to full-time Christian service.

The example of my savior, Jesus, finally wrecked me. His own genealogy contained people with questionable backgrounds, and details of his birth appeared sketchy. He chose uneducated, ordinary disciples who would never meet my so-called standards to build his church. Even the apostle Paul, who claimed the perfect spiritual pedigree (Phil. 3:4–7), admitted God called him by grace (Gal. 1:14–15) and not because of his credentials or zeal.

God hated my pride, and I learned to recognize and hate it too. God says, "Whoever has haughty eyes and a proud heart, I will not tolerate" (Ps. 101:5), and "All our righteous acts are like filthy rags" (Isa. 64:6). God "opposes the proud" (James 4:6). And Jesus spoke most harshly to the self-righteous Pharisees compared to anyone else (Matt. 23), directly criticizing their false spirituality.

Slowly, I recognized my teammates' "brokenness" did not disqualify them for ministry, but rather, enhanced their ability to serve God. They were humble and dependent on him in ways I was not. Their experiences produced compassionate hearts that understood the gift of God's forgiveness and grace which they then extended to others. And these same people rallied around me and offered me hope and comfort as my own pain came to light.

Over time, I confessed my need for forgiveness and grace. I grew more sympathetic to the plight of others, less apt to give pat advice, more aware of the variety of ways God disciples his children, and more willing to serve the brokenhearted. Smashing my pride has been and will continue to be a life-long journey which began in earnest through the lives of my broken and beautiful teammates.

Read

Read Mark 2:13–17; Luke 18:9–14.
What "standards" do you have that God might be challenging?

Recount

Call to mind a time when God revealed your judgmental standards and, despite them, you experienced his grace in appointing you to serve him. In what forum might you share this testimony?

Respond

Father God, I repent of my pride that thinks I'm better than others because of my background, education, choices, family of origin, or any other marker. Continue to teach me to see all your creatures as image-bearers equally valued and loved. Give me a heart that elevates others above myself. Help me to serve others, not as though I'm doing someone a favor, but rather, joyfully and with a humble heart.

20

Prone to Complain

Jesus Demonstrates How to Shine Like Stars

Do everything without grumbling or arguing, so that you may become blameless and pure, "children of God without fault in a warped and crooked generation." Then you will shine among them like stars in the sky.
Philippians 2:14–15

"I took the boys to the playground. But all the stares, comments, and questions about where I am from eventually got to me, so we came home early," I complained to my husband.

"We went to watch the traditional arts festival, but as usual, our family ended up being more of an attraction than the performers. The pushing and questions were so annoying. One woman even pulled my poor son's nose really hard, fascinated by its size and shape," I grumbled in my family letter.

"A guy I've never seen before came by the house trying to sell a sticker to place on our front door. He claimed he was a Christian and that I should help him out because he was such a good friend of Mark's. I felt anger, not knowing if he spoke truthfully and, at the same time, felt guilty if I didn't help him," I fussed in my journal to the Lord.

"A delivery truck backed into my parked car at the grocery store. Why are we stuck with the repair bill? Just because we're from America, they think we're made of money," I murmured to my teammates.

I was tired of being an outsider in a foreign land. Tired of feeling cheated. Tired of the stares and questions. It was so easy to grumble and complain. About everything and everyone. I complained about the immaturity of our national team. I grumbled when my team leader asked me to take on a responsibility that I felt interrupted my work. I murmured when colleagues insisted they didn't say something I distinctly remembered.

When my negativity got out of hand, the Holy Spirit convicted me of my sin of complaining and my penchant for focusing on the difficult aspects of our expat life. A verse I had memorized as a child sprang to mind. Above our kitchen sink, my mother had fastened a card with the command to do all things without grumbling.

I find the context of this verse most interesting. First the passage exhorts me to imitate Jesus (Phil. 2:5–7) by not exerting my rights, but instead humbling myself, putting aside my own interests, and valuing others above myself (Phil. 2:3–4). Then the author explains that I can live selflessly like this because I cooperate with God. I live out my salvation, and he works in me "to will and to act in order to fulfill his good purposes" (Phil. 2:12–13).

Directly after this reminder that God is working in me, we find the command to not grumble or argue so that we "may become blameless and pure children of God without fault" (Phil. 2:15). Herein lay my motivation. If I ceased complaining, then I would shine as a bright star in a spiritually dark world (Phil. 2:15)! Isn't that why I came here in the first place?

Since God was working in me, he could help me be content in my context and trust him with my team and my life. More than that, he empowered me to imitate Christ and live humbly and selflessly. And by doing this, I could show my community what a pure and blameless child of God looks like. Boy, did I have a long way to go!

I confessed my complaining spirit about the culture. I repented of my grumbling about the team. I confessed my negative attitude. I then concentrated on looking for the good around me. I asked God to work in me to love sincerely, assume the best, offer hope, and build others up (Rom. 12:10–12).

I truly wanted my light to shine brightly in this spiritually dark place, so the next time I was tempted to grumble, I paused—and chose instead to imitate Jesus.

Read

Open your Bible to Philippians 2:1–18.
What is God saying to you through these verses?

Recount

Think back to a time when God helped you to not complain. Who can you tell about this progress in your spiritual growth?

Respond

Precious Jesus, thank you for your beautiful example of how to humble myself and consider others first. Help me to not complain about my circumstances and those I work with. Teach me how to set aside my interests and instead value those I serve and live among.

21

Give It Now

Our Good Father Gives Us Good Gifts

Which of you, if your son asks for bread, will give him a stone? Or if he asks for a fish, will give him a snake? If you, then, though you are evil, know how to give good gifts to your children, how much more will your Father in heaven give good gifts to those who ask him!
Matthew 7:9–11

One day while at the pool, my son ran to me screaming, "Moooooom!" He sounded so distraught I thought he was badly hurt.

Worried, I ran to him and picked him up. "What's the matter? Are you in pain?" I asked.

"I'm hungry," he wailed.

I calmed him down and gave him his sandwich, reassuring him I would always take care of his needs. He would never go hungry under my watch.

"Why did you cry so loudly?" I asked after he was quiet.

"I saw my brother eating his ice cream," he explained.

Ice cream was our typical after-meal treat, so my son felt sure he had missed out on his meal—but mostly his dessert. He had not stopped to consider that his brother had already eaten his lunch, whereas he had been so busy playing he had lost track of the time.

His over-the-top reaction took me aback. I wondered where such fear came from. Had I been a capricious mother to cause him to think I would withhold food from him? Had I given him any reason to doubt I would not provide? Of course not.

I chalked it up to childish insecurity. But it got me thinking. *Am I at times like this? Do I run screaming to my heavenly Father, certain that he isn't going to give me what I need? Am I afraid he's also withholding extra rewards?*

Around that time we needed a visa (an annual ritual), and I filled my journal pages with my worry and concern. I begged God to continue to provide the permission to reside in the country. I made up scenarios in my mind about how he could answer our need. And I insisted he do it when it was convenient for me. *Yikes. I was indeed acting like an insecure child who believed that God would refuse to give me what I asked for.*

But I knew God isn't like that. Just like my son's lunch was ready and waiting for him to enjoy (along with dessert), my Lord had my provision ready and waiting for me to claim. I knew how to give a good meal to my son. How much more would God give me what I asked for (Matt. 7:11)?

I continued to meditate on the truth that I could ask God for what I needed (Matt. 7:7–8) and that he knew what I needed before I even asked (Matt. 6:8). I confessed my childishness to God. In the same way I responded to my son, God seemed to reply in kind: *Don't you think I have your visa ready for you? Why do you keep screaming at me to give it to you? Trust me. As I always provide for you, I will do so again.*

Read

Peruse Psalm 145:15–16; Matthew 7:7–8; 2 Corinthians 9:8; Philippians 4:19; James 1:17.
What do these verses tell you about God's response to your requests?

Recount

Recount a time when God had his provision ready for you despite your impatient demand.

Respond

Father God, I confess my impatience and lack of trust, believing you will withhold goodness from me, instead of trusting that you are a good Father who loves to give good gifts to your children. You will not give me a "snake" when I have asked for a "fish" (Matt. 7:9).

22

Why Not Me?

God Enables Us to Rejoice with Others

Love does not envy.
1 Corinthians 13:4

When I moved overseas, two of my siblings remained unmarried. When the news arrived that my youngest sister planned to tie the knot, I wanted desperately to attend the ceremony. But then a struggle began. *Should I go? Can I go? What about the expense?* I felt such an extravagant trip was impossible. Mainly because we had little discretionary money, but also because of the precedent set by my family of origin.

My parents spent their donated funds carefully and sparingly. They took seriously Jesus's promise that "everyone who has left houses or brothers or sisters or father or mother or wife or children or fields for [his] sake will receive a hundred times as much and will inherit eternal life" (Matt. 19:29). This promise provided some comfort when distance, timing, and money necessitated denying ourselves attendance at special extended family events. (I had already missed the other sister's wedding as well as my grandmother's funeral.)

But my parents seemed to imply, albeit unintentionally, that we did not have permission to even consider such pleasures. I knew that following God to work overseas included sacrifices of all kinds, yet I also believed that God didn't ask me to deny myself every delight.

While I wrestled with this decision and discussed values

about money, desire, and budget with my husband, I learned that my teammate had been gifted a ticket to attend her friend's wedding in the U.S. Immediately the fingers of envy wound around my heart. *It's not fair. Why can she go and not me? I want to enjoy a trip home too,* I cried to the Lord.

Envy is a resentful desire and contempt toward those who have what we don't. It distorts how we view them, making it easier to criticize and harder to celebrate with them. It deteriorates and rots our souls (Prov. 14:30). It certainly isn't loving (1 Cor. 13:4).

I didn't want to let envy take control of me. I didn't want to begrudge the gift God had given my teammate or let my own desire twist my opinion of her. Instead, I wanted to celebrate and rejoice with her that she got to participate in such a memorable event (Rom. 12:15; 1 Cor. 12:26).

My husband and I began to pray. We had some Christmas gift money that we could put towards a plane fare, but it wasn't enough. We asked God to provide the remainder—a specific amount—to indicate if I could go to the wedding. I surrendered my desire to the Lord. I would accept his direction.

The days passed and nothing happened. Perhaps the Lord had shut the door. But as soon as I had resigned to not going, a letter arrived from the bride-to-be. She listed all the various events our family had missed over the years. She expressed just how hard it was for her that, once again, her loved ones must miss an important milestone. She wanted me there, so she offered to give me her Christmas bonus to assist in purchasing my ticket. It was the exact amount we had asked the Lord to provide.

I flew to the U.S. To this day, I'm glad I attended the wedding. It meant so much to my sister and me to be present as she said her vows. To top it off, my sons made special memories with their dad at home.

Following Christ sometimes means giving up something I really want to do, but it does not require denial of every pleasure in life. I learned to let God grant my desires his way, while not envying the choices others make.

Read

Look up and meditate on the verses above.
What experience have you been denied that someone else has enjoyed?
How have you resisted the pangs of envy?

Recount

Write a story about a time when God convicted you of envy and granted your desire in his own way. Who might benefit from your example?

Respond

Heavenly Father, show me where I have allowed envy to begin to rot my soul. Teach me to rejoice when you give good gifts to others. I present my requests and desires to you and surrender the outcome. Please give me what you know I need and grant the desires you are delighted to fulfill.

23

Irritated

God Helps Us to Forbear

Be completely humble and gentle; be patient,
bearing with one another in love.
Ephesians 4:2

Our national team of evangelists gathered for their weekly meeting. My husband opened the meeting with an invitation: "Let's spend some time sharing something the Lord has been teaching us."

Nella spoke up first and shared a truth she had gleaned from her morning quiet time. I don't remember the content of her testimony, but apparently she addressed a pertinent issue. Her teammate, Ernest, immediately accused her of deliberately choosing that verse to rebuke him specifically.

As soon as I heard this interchange, I too felt convicted. But not by Nella's testimony—rather, Ernest's reaction to it. *I'm responding exactly like Ernest,* I realized. *I'm believing a lie.*

I had been struggling for many months with my slow progress in ministry. I second-guessed my abilities and my methods and compared myself to my teammates. Where I lacked confidence, they seemed sure and successful.

Soon, I began to dread their reports. If they shared about their work or a strategy they had implemented, I presumed they were pressuring me to imitate them. As Ernest had responded to Nella's testimony, I interpreted their words as personal rebuke. I believed (falsely) that they had an agenda behind their words, that every story they told was directed at me. Consequently, I stopped showing interest in their ministry or asking for advice. A few times I lashed out in self-defense and frustration.

I must stop assuming my teammates' motives, I confessed to the Lord. *Furthermore, I have allowed their voices to overshadow yours. Instead, I will show interest in their stories and weigh their advice against your voice. While I can learn from them, ultimately it is you I obey. And you do not condemn me for the way I conduct my ministry.*

Besides listening to God above others, I wish now that I could go back to my young self and tell her to simply forbear (Eph. 4:2). My teammates' actions were not sinful. They were not unkind or domineering. To genuinely love them, I would accept them and overlook their quirks rather than focus on the things that irritated me. Because, of course, they had to choose to do the same with me.

My friend and author, Carol Dowsett, describes forbearance like this:

> Forbearance is the loving act of preemptive forgiveness. It decides ahead of time that verbal jabs and unwitting irritations will not take root. It gives the benefit of the doubt and presumes the best.[21]

My teammates had to regularly forbear my flippant words and lack of attention (and all my idiosyncrasies and rough edges). I can't say I mastered my irritation, but over time I did gain confidence in my ministry.

Read

Check out Deuteronomy 9:27; 30:20; Proverbs 12:16; 19:11; John 10:27; 16:13; Colossians 3:13.
What is God saying to you through these verses about forbearing with others and listening to him?

Recount

Think of a time when you were able to forbear with others because you heard God's voice above all else. To whom might you relay this story?

Respond

Lord God, help me listen to your voice, while at the same time affirm others, reach out, not portray irritation, be genuine in my praise, and show love. Teach and enable me to forbear with my fellow humans. Help me to humbly remember that I annoy and bug other people and that they must put up with me. As I desire them to overlook my faults, help me to overlook the behaviors, words, and attitudes of others who frustrate, vex, and irritate me.

24

Idol of the Heart

God Sets Us Free from Lies

The poor, deluded fool feeds on ashes. He trusts something that can't help him at all. Yet he cannot bring himself to ask, "Is this idol that I'm holding in my hand a lie?"
Isaiah 44:20 NLT

Living in Indonesia brought me face to face with idols for the first time. I mean actual idols—carved manmade images of gods with bulging eyes, giant teeth, and bulbous stomachs. Grotesque scary creatures were stationed inside and outside homes and temples and carried on poles high above the crowd during parades. Daily offerings were spread over the sidewalks with tiny streams of incense. Artwork and dances depicted gods, gods, and more gods. Idol worship was indeed alive and well in that corner of the world.

An idol can be defined as anything we value more than God, that draws our attention and worship away from him, or that we expect will give us what only he can. Jonah succinctly states it best:

> Those who cling to worthless idols turn away from God's love for them. (Jonah 2:8)

The prophet Isaiah emphasizes over and over the uselessness and foolishness of trusting in idols. Because they are crafted out of ordinary materials by spiritually blind humans, they cannot give counsel, answer questions, foretell the future, lift our burdens, or save us. In fact, these hand-crafted objects lie, promising what they cannot deliver (Isa. 41:22–24, 28–29; 44:9–20; 45:20; 46:1–2).

The manmade idols around me were easy to identify as worthless and weak. However, because I didn't set out daily offerings to carved figurines, it was harder to recognize the idol I actually set up in my own heart. Through a study of Rachel, the wife of the Hebrew patriarch, Jacob, the Lord revealed my idol.

Rachel could not bear children. She blamed her husband for this hardship and demanded, "Give me children or I'll die" (Gen. 30:1), expecting him to do something only God could do. She then took matters into her own hands and spent her life in envy of her sister's ability to bear sons, manipulating and clinging to her own household gods (Gen. 31:19). Her normal desire to be a mother became the idol that overtook her heart.

Similar to Rachel, my desire for my husband overtook my heart. I denied myself other deep friendships thinking I only needed him. I expected him to give me all the love, attention, and intimacy I craved. I also looked to him to provide all the fun, adventure, open doors to ministry, provision, advice, and guidance.

Therapist and author Leslie Vernick says, "When we must have these things for our well-being, when we feel God is insufficient, then these desires have become idols and have taken first place in our heart. These loves, no matter how good and legitimate they are, compromise our intimacy with God."[22]

I had placed my husband on my heart's throne until he finally fell off, utterly unable to meet my expectations. (He didn't want to be my idol anyway.) When the reality of my deprivation hit home, I was devastated, yet it revealed the wrongful place I had tried to make him occupy. The pain of my unmet needs forced me to acknowledge that I had not named the Lord as the "lover of my soul." He had been replaced by my earthly lover, and that man had failed me.

I confessed my idolatry (1 Cor. 10:14) and turned to God (Isa. 44:22). I started letting him be my first love (Rev. 2:4). I studied his character and adjusted my beliefs based on what I learned. I exchanged my transactional view of him—the one that expected reward for my good behavior—for one of grace. I discovered a good God who valued me as his beautiful daughter and lavished his love on me. I could trust him with my whole heart. He would satisfy my needs. He was enough (Ps. 145; Rom. 8:35–39).

Read

Look up and meditate on some of the verses referenced above. What might have turned you away from God's love? Why?

Recount

Remember and tell someone about a time when God set you free from an idol that had captured your heart.

Respond

Mighty One, this thing I'm holding onto is a lie. It cannot answer my questions, give me advice, or tell me what my future holds. You alone are God. You can carry me and lift my burdens. Please recapture my heart.

Week Five

Liturgy for Navigating Crises

We've experienced so many crises, Lord,
that they're becoming routine.
How can we endure another?

Why does something always seem to happen?
Maybe this is just life, and crises happen everywhere—
a medical evacuation, an unexpected illness
a devastating storm, a life-threatening accident,
a riot, destruction, death.

We are crushed, distracted, on high alert,
running on adrenaline.
Some are fighting, others fleeing or freezing.
We crave rest but have to press on—
to file government paperwork,
shield and protect children,
make endless calls, update reports,
care for wounded ones, and get much-needed sleep.

Our team is hurting. We need hope.
Help us see this through your eyes,
not just our narrow vision of right now, right here.
Send us help when we need it,
counselors and professionals who know how to
advise, debrief, and comfort, and restore our bodies and souls.

Bind us together in love,
give the strong one compassion for the weak.
May we cast our grief and anxiety on you
and not on those around us.
When we allow ourselves to process the emotions,
they are less likely to come out sideways
against those we truly love.

I reach out to you, Father, I trust you.
You are good, and I will praise you
even as life shifts once again.
I accept both the good and the bad,
I trust that you intend to work in some way through this pain.

You are our refuge and strength,
An ever-present help in the midst of this trouble.
I seek you because you are not far off.

You said these waters I'm passing through
will not sweep me away
and the fire will not burn me.
But I have been swept away, I have been burned.
Your Word says you were with me even then,
even though I suffered and those around me are still suffering.

My soul is weary with sorrow;
strengthen me with promises from your Word,
continue the work you have begun,
help us shine brightly in the tragedy,
and comfort others with the comfort we receive.

Please stop every effort of the enemy to rob, kill,
and destroy through this crisis.
Renew our strength, Lord, so that we can run
and not grow weary, walk and not faint.

Even in this "routine crisis" you protect once again,
and you get the glory.

Amen.[23]

25

Up in Smoke

God is Our Strong Tower

The name of the Lord is a strong tower;
The righteous run to it and are safe.
Proverbs 18:10 (NKJV)

While on vacation in early 2000, I crafted my annual goals. I sensed the Lord through Isaiah 43:19 asking me, "Are you willing to let me do something new this year?"

"Yes," I wrote, "but you must make it very plain. I confess my love of safety, comfort, familiarity, and the haven of home. Lord, you will have to give the desire, motivation, guidance, strength, and results."

Back at home one week later, we commenced homeschool with renewed vigor. I wanted to get into routine even with added guests. A former teammate had arrived the day before to spend two weeks with us. He and Mark headed to the airport to pick up yet another guest—our area director.

As the boys worked on their assignments, I started a letter to my mother:

> Today is January 17th. There is a group of folks demonstrating in the governor's enclosure this morning. Recently reports of Christians killing Muslims in other parts of the country have incited them, and they are protesting. We have been told to stay at home, but we are not terribly alarmed, just being careful.

We were accustomed to hearing reports of this kind of "tit-for-tat." While on paper Indonesia allows freedom for five religions, in practice the majority dominates. A simple rumor could incite crowds to anger and retaliation.

I discontinued my letter when the men returned from the airport. "We saw smoke," they reported. "Several churches are on fire." Throughout the day, the violence continued to escalate from burning churches to homes and businesses of Christians. We discovered later that this was not an ad hoc retaliatory mob, but rather about 20,000 organized demonstrators given specific targets throughout the city and the whole island.

At noon, Nella called in a panic. A Muslim friend had warned her, "After they burn down the churches, they will find all the Christians and chase you out. Flee while you can." Taking this threat seriously, she left the island in the first wave of thousands who eventually evacuated.

The afternoon continued with phone calls, discussions, prayer, and growing anxiety until finally, over supper, our team realized the violence wasn't dying down. We decided to leave our homes and seek protection in the tourist district.

Grabbing a bag, I frantically threw in clothing, schoolbooks, and a few toys that had just arrived from grandparents that day. Then because of the uncertainty of the situation, I filled a second bag with precious photo albums, important papers, credit cards, passports, and my address book. I believe God gave me wisdom in what I selected in my hurry.

A quick fifteen minutes later, we were on the road. During the thirty-minute ride to the hotel, our guest prayed, and my son asked to sing. We launched into a scripture song (based on Proverbs 18:10) sung during church the day before:

> The name of the Lord is a strong tower, the righteous run into it and they are saved.

That was the first of many times this specific verse came to mind in the ensuing forty-eight hours. We encountered no one on the roads, arriving safely at the hotel ahead of the rioters who crowded the same road later that evening. God answered our cries for help.

The next day, a steady queue of helicopters and vans shuttled tourists, expatriates, and nationals to the safety of the neighboring island while we watched, wondering why we did not fly away as well. We spent countless hours on the phone notifying our prayer teams and searching for local Christian friends who were likely running for their lives. As the day wore on, our teammates successfully helped one of these couples join us at the hotel.

When we all met together that afternoon to assess our situation, I broke down. I wept for the potential loss of my physical home, my belongings, my settled routine, and the peaceful life my children enjoyed. As far as I knew, it was all going up in smoke.

I wanted to abandon it all, get on a plane, and fly to the U.S. Instead, I sensed the Lord asking me to offer everything to him—my home, my life, my ministry, and the island we had come to know and love. Was this the new thing God wanted to do?

As I cried, his perspective came, and I chose to surrender. Peace flooded my heart. Once again God reminded me not to hold tightly to those things which seemingly provide security and safety. My security was in him alone. He truly was my strong tower.[24]

Read

Read Psalm 61:3; 121:1–8; 2 Thessalonians 3:2–3; 2 Timothy 4:17–18. What do these verses tell you about your place of safety?

Recount

Describe a time when life was going up in smoke around you and God proved to be your strong tower. Who can you tell?

Respond

Precious Father, thank you that all these years later, you remain my strong tower. Whether the destruction around me comes from physical danger or emotional onslaught, I remain safe with you. While you might not remove the threat, you will enable me to walk through it.

26

Women and Children First

Jesus Gives Peace Amid Fear

Peace I leave with you; my peace I give you.
I do not give to you as the world gives.
Do not let your hearts be troubled and do not be afraid.
John 14:27

"Wake up! Gather your belongings and meet in the hotel lobby!" A heavy banging on the door aroused us from the beds we had just settled into. "The mob is coming up the road!"

This time my husband panicked. He quickly filled a bag half full only to spill its contents on the floor. "What are we going to do?" he cried in dismay.

It was my turn to be calm. "We're going to pack, wake the boys, and take our bags to the lobby." Though still frantic, we got things together and joined several hundred hotel guests to await next steps. There we received the news we had dreaded—the mob that had burned churches and ransacked houses on the island for the last two days was heading our way.

Despite the danger, we were with our dear teammates. We comforted each other and helped with all our children, while laughing and making jokes about our situation. An hour later, word came that the police halted the mob a few miles away.

Although momentarily safe, the hotel manager realized he could not keep us all protected nor feed us indefinitely. He decided to evacuate all guests by shuttle bus up the coast to then board a jet boat to the neighboring island.

"Women and children first," the assistant manager called out when the first shuttle vans arrived.

"Are you serious?" I thought, "Have you been watching

Titanic?" Nonetheless, my two sons and I complied, stuffing ourselves into a bus with other women and children. My husband then joined the men in several smaller vans, and the convoy headed out for the ten-minute ride.

As the old diesel engine of our over-loaded van grunted up the first hill, the lighter vans quickly passed us by. Thirty minutes later, after praying the vehicle over each hill, I knew the driver was lost. Eventually he turned around. During the whole trek I held both my teammates' hands while our children napped on our laps. I kept praying, singing the "Strong Tower" song and reciting, "My peace I give you. Do not let your hearts be troubled and do not be afraid" (John 14:27). I knew that we were in God's hands—the safest place possible.

When the men arrived at the dock and realized the women and children were no longer "first" (in spite of the hotel manager's best intentions), they sent a search vehicle. We eventually joined the men—in last place—but in time to catch the boat.

The scene was surreal—escaping violence and destruction aimed at the children of God on a beautiful, starry night. Enjoying an "adventure" with friends while fleeing the anger of enemies.

The large capacity jet boat arrived around 1:30 a.m. Due to high waves and lack of a real dock, loading all five hundred passengers and their luggage took three more hours. At one point, the captain discontinued loading until the waves subsided. However, we boarded early and the children soon fell asleep. We arrived at the hotel around 6 a.m. and went to bed an hour later. That same jet boat headed back to the island, completing three trips that day and evacuating around 1200 people.

Once again, God had spared me and my loved ones from violence and provided a way of escape, but I still had to maneuver the unknown and the added emotional strain. We had no idea if we'd ever be able to return to our home or continue our ministry. While I awaited the outcome of this senseless destruction, God's Word gave me strength to live in limbo, to explain hard things to my children, and later, to help those who had suffered far worse than we had.

Read

Peruse Proverbs 18:10; Isaiah 9:6; Matthew 5:9; John 14:27. What do these verses tell you about God's peace in the midst of fear?

Recount

Recount to a loved one a time when God gave you peace when you were afraid.

Respond

Precious Jesus, thank you that as you protected us all those years ago, you will continue to care for us during current and future troubling and uncertain times. Give me your peace and help me not to be afraid.

27

Unlikely Provision

God Does More Than We Imagine

> *Now to him who is able to do immeasurably more than all we ask or imagine, according to his power that is at work within us.*
> *Ephesians 3:20*

In advance of the dawn of the new millennium, speculation abounded about whether a computer programming shortcut (a two-digit date format) would cause havoc in the electronic, specifically the banking, world. In response to this possibility, known as Y2K, my husband took a few extra precautions. A few days before the clock struck midnight on the new year, Mark withdrew a significant amount of money from the bank—just in case.

In the end, January 1 arrived without incident. We stashed the cash. Then the uprising of January 17 erupted around us. We retrieved the cash. God, in his foresight, knew that 20,000 Muslims would go on a four-day rioting spree systematically burning and ransacking fourteen churches and at least two hundred homes and businesses of Christians on the island and displacing 10,000 Christians (figures vary according to the report).[25] He knew banks would be closed in the aftermath and ATMs inoperable. We were so thankful that we had this ready money.

After we evacuated to the neighboring island, looting and vandalism continued for two more weeks. We set up a temporary home in a hotel suite, and I tried to maintain routine for our family by continuing homeschooling.

Our helper, Sue, later informed us that at the same time we

were settling into our interim lodgings, a mob came up our street and inquired about us (with the intent to burn homes owned by Christians). Her husband told the mob, truthfully, that the home was owned by a Hindu family (we only rented it). The neighbor verified the information, and the crowd moved on.

The following day, they heard rumors that the mob might return, so they began to pack up possessions they deemed precious to us and prepared to hoist these things over the back wall to a neighbor's home. Fortunately, the mob never returned. God used our loyal friends to defend our home and our belongings. However, eleven Christian families in our neighborhood experienced the theft of their belongings and the burning of their houses.

My husband and our teammates focused on finding our national co-workers. Once they were located, we purchased tickets so they could leave the island. After their evacuation, we provided food, clothing, and shelter for as many as we could.

We debriefed each one. While we could fall back on our status as "tourists," they had been the target of the hatred. Their lives had been in danger. We listened aghast to their stories of escape, hiding out in forests and rice paddies,[26] sheltering in police barracks, hearing gun shots, and eating ramen noodles three times a day. Many lost their homes. Some had their belongings strewn on the streets. And all their possessions were burned by angry crowds of Muslims chanting "*Jihad*!" (holy war) and "Death to Christians."

As I prayed for my hurting friends, verse after verse from the book of Isaiah reminded me of God's protection and salvation, of his restoration of his people, and his call to be his witnesses.

> So do not fear, for I am with you; do not be dismayed, for I am your God. I will strengthen you and help you; I will uphold you with my righteous right hand. (Isa. 41:10)

> Do not tremble, do not be afraid. . . . You are my witnesses. Is there any God besides me? No, there is no other Rock; I know not one. (Isa. 44:8)

> In repentance and rest is your salvation, in quietness and trust is your strength. (Isa. 30:15)

> He has sent me to bind up the brokenhearted, to proclaim freedom for the captives and release from darkness for the prisoners. (Isa. 61:1)

The senseless destruction was heart-wrenching. Even though surrounded by chaos we also heard amazing stories of God's protection and mercy. The Y2K hype ended up being a means of provision for us, enabling us to meet the needs of our local friends. Months later, after everything settled down, several supporting churches reimbursed everyone's expenses—ours, our teammates', and our local partners'. The emails, phone calls, and generous financial gifts from so many encouraged us greatly.

Read

Meditate on the verses above.
What do they tell you about God's provision, protection, and mighty power?

Recount

Tell someone about a time when God provided for you in ways you could not have imagined.

Respond

O God my Rock and Provider, I am reminded that apocalyptic warnings and end-time predictions are nothing new. Help me to release their control over me by not giving in to fear, but instead trusting in you. Thank you for the strength and peace that you provide when I fix my thoughts on you, not on speculations. As you worked immeasurably more than I could have imagined all those years ago, I affirm that you are the same God who will continue to care for me.

28

In the Arms of Jesus

God Carries Us Close to His Heart

He tends his flock like a shepherd: He gathers the lambs in his arms and carries them close to his heart; he gently leads those that have young.
Isaiah 40:11

Three weeks after we evacuated, we returned to our home. Though a bit reticent, I felt such relief to be back. On my desk I found my unfinished letter to my parents dated January 17, the day the riots broke out. My last words on the unfinished page read, "We are not terribly alarmed, just being careful."

On February 9, I picked up where I had left off:

> Funny, we weren't alarmed—YET!
>
> Coming home from the airport, everything looked pretty normal, even quieter. But we see destroyed buildings and gutted homes with their insides all black. How devastating, especially, to see churches and the homes of our dear friends burned. Our son said it made him sad to see the houses.
>
> Things are not safe at night. Folks are fearful of robbery, and rumors are flying of continued unrest. (Our neighborhood has recruited night watchmen who clang on the electricity poles to reassure us (!) all is safe.) I am packing a few bags for emergency getaway if necessary. There is still the chance that the president will not be able to control his military, and the country may go to war. So we need great wisdom to discern when we should leave, if at all.
>
> Nella also returned. She is spending tonight with us as it is

not safe for her to be alone in her house. Earlier she was frightened by a neighbor who told her not to open her curtains or let folks know she is here. And our other national co-workers are not yet ready to come back. One couple's home was completely destroyed and all their belongings burned. Another's was ransacked and damaged but can be repaired. Still others did not lose any material possessions. But all fled to safety on other islands.

We are getting mixed reactions from the local people. Some seem to think the riots were no big deal. They believe there was not much damage, and only a few people evacuated. Some even blame Christians and think they deserved to be chased off the island. Others seem remorseful but not really embarrassed or repentant. Then there are those who have felt genuine concern for their Christian friends. One Muslim friend of Nella's was in tears when she heard Nella was safe. Others phoned to let her know they were concerned, they looked for her, and they are ashamed about what their countrymen did.

Much healing and restoration needs to take place, and it would be such a testimony if believers can return with love and forgiveness and demonstrate that they will not fight back.

I feel weak and inadequate. One verse in particular has guided me: "God has not given us a spirit of fear but of power and of love and of a sound mind" (2 Tim. 1:7 NKJV). Instead of fear, I need love to forgive those who have done this evil and caused the destruction. I need a sound mind to discern the truth amidst the daily rumors, to keep fearful scenarios from my thoughts, and to know when it is no longer safe to stay here. And I need power to do this task we have been called to do, to be his witnesses.

We picked up our mail today. There were two letters from you, Mom. The one written on January 2 had a footnote: "I see you in the arms of Jesus Christ." Do you remember writing that? Well, it was a very special message meant for today. We are in his arms here and that is a very safe place. Please pray for peace and contentment to live day by day in this constant state of flux and unrest.

What comfort it was to realize my mother had prayed for our protection before we needed it. My family, team, and I had been gathered into God's arms and carried close to his heart.

Read

Check out Psalm 46:1; 91:4, 9–12; Isaiah 26:3; Matthew 23:37. How do these verses comfort you as you face risk and danger?

Recount

Tell an account of a time when God carried you close to his heart during a season of risk.

Respond

Unchangeable God, once again, I need love for those who cause my distress, a sound mind to filter all the voices around me, and power to do what you have asked of me. Thank you for carrying me close to your heart in the middle of current unrest and uncertainty.

29

Rumors and Risk

God Takes Care of Us When We Face Opposition

Are not two sparrows sold for a penny? Yet not one of them will fall to the ground outside your Father's care. And even the very hairs of your head are all numbered. So don't be afraid; you are worth more than many sparrows.
Matthew 10:29–31

After the riots, business owners of all persuasions on the island met together and agreed that the riots had taken a huge toll on the island economically and socially. Therefore, they would never again allow outsiders to come and incite violence on their peaceful island. Fortunately, no Christians retaliated, and the riots were put behind them as they began to rebuild.

However, despite this pledge to peace, rumors of another purported attack surfaced and spread. We learned that spreading rumors after a time of unrest is a common tactic to keep people in fear. This particularly affected our local friends. One threat kept our local co-workers immobilized for days. Some considered leaving the island for good. Others retreated, afraid to boldly share the gospel.

As their mentor, I turned to Jesus's commissioning address in Matthew 10 for insight. Jesus told his disciples not to be surprised at the risks involved in their commission. After all, they were like sheep among wolves. They followed a shepherd and depended on him for their very lives while facing evil and cruel enemies.

Jesus clearly spelled out the risks involved in ministry. His followers would be arrested and tried before civil and religious leaders, persecuted, hated by all including their own family, physically beaten, and maybe even put to death. He, their teacher and example, had been insulted, misunderstood, and eventually killed. How could they, as his followers, expect any less?

In response to these risks, Jesus told them to stand firm in their allegiance to him, for he was their priority above all else. Even though persecuted, they should acknowledge him publicly and proclaim the coming kingdom. When they experienced persecution, they should be both wise and innocent in their approach.

Jesus also knew that his followers were human and prone to respond poorly. He warned them against fear and worry, disowning Christ, loving family more than Christ, and not taking up our crosses to follow him.

Despite these ministry risks, Jesus promised help. The disciples need not worry about what to say when facing persecutors, for the Spirit would speak through them. If they stood firm to the end, they would be saved, acknowledged before God, and rewarded in heaven. Thus, they did not need to fear because God cared about them so much that he knew the exact number of hairs on their head—they were that valuable to him.

Like the disciples, my national co-workers had experienced consequences from following Christ. They left family behind. They trusted God for daily provisions. They were hated by their neighbors, chased from their homes, stripped of their belongings, and forced to resettle from scratch. But God had not forgotten them, as theologian N. T. Wright reminds us:

> You are worth more than a great many sparrows; so rest assured that God knows and cares about the details of your life, even as you face the temptations and dangers which so easily surround you. Followers of Jesus are bound to expect attacks at all levels. But they should also learn that the one they are serving is stronger than the strongest opponent they will ever meet.[27]

My co-workers and I prayed that we would be ready to face whatever else came our way. Our ministry would continue to experience opposition—that had been promised. But we could also claim Jesus's promises that he would take care of us.

Read

Skim Matthew 10.
What cost have you paid for sharing the good news of the kingdom of God?
Which of God's promises do you need to cling to today?

Recount

Recall a time when God took care of you even though you faced persecution or opposition. Tell someone who needs to hear about God's promises of care.

Respond

Heavenly Father, the task of sharing about your kingdom is tough, frightening, and certainly not safe. I have never experienced what your disciples faced nor what my local friends faced. My service to you seems so small and insignificant. But you say I need to be ready to face any risks of serving you. Embolden my weak heart today, I pray.

30

Through a Child's Eyes

God Protects Us

> *In the same way your Father in heaven is not willing that any of these little ones should perish.*
> *Matthew 18:14*

After the riots, people asked us how our sons were doing. They behaved normally and didn't exhibit any signs of trauma (that I could see). However, three years later our son completed an assignment in school and wrote about his experiences during the evacuation. At that time, I learned about some of his feelings. I share his composition with his permission:

> In the year 2000 in Indonesia I was having fun with my brother (surprisingly) when we somehow heard the news. I was seven years old when this happened. The Muslims were burning down Christians' houses because they wanted to revolt. My Mom said we had to go to the Holiday Inn. At first I wasn't afraid. I thought the riot would stop and everything would be okay.
>
> I was wrong.
>
> When we got to the Holiday Inn, we checked in, found our room, and went to the pool to play with our friends. We stayed at the inn for a few days and had a smashing time.
>
> Then real problems arose.
>
> The riot was getting worse. We couldn't stay much longer. I started getting scared. I had pictures in my brain of our house engulfed in flames. That night my family and my

> friend's family decided that we were going to [the next island].
>
> We waited for hours for the bus to arrive. When it finally did, we got on and slept a little.
>
> When we got to the port, we waited longer for the boat to arrive. A lot of other people were there, and the air was filled with the smell of smoke. When the ship arrived, we boarded and went to sleep.
>
> We arrived the next day. My family got on a taxi and drove to a nice hotel. We stayed there for about two weeks, while my Dad went back home for a day to get toys. Would he come back? He did.
>
> When we finally could go back, we all went back on the same boat we took. After about three weeks away from my home, I was happy to get home.

As a parent, I didn't always know what my sons felt or how they processed the events we faced. I also did not yet understand trauma and how to debrief children. But I prayed for them constantly. I asked God to shield their eyes from firsthand violence and to protect them from evil, and in this instance he did.

I knew I could not always protect my children as I wanted to. After all, not every child is spared from experiencing violence as my sons were. But I could keep praying and trusting that God cared for my family. He showed up in big and small ways if I only paid attention. I resolved to keep looking for his fingerprints and remembering the ways he intervened and cared.

Read

Open your Bible to Isaiah 49:25; 54:13; Matthew 18:1–14; 1 John 5:18–20. How do these verses help you trust God with your children's protection?

Recount

When has God protected your children? Tell them as a reminder of God's faithfulness.

Respond

Gracious Father, thank you for shielding my sons from witnessing violence during those uncertain weeks. Thank you that they had friends to bring a sense of adventure to the stress. Thank you for giving me wisdom to care for them during that troubling time. I pray for moms facing crises. Give them wisdom and strength. Help them to trust you so their children will catch their faith, not their fear.

Week Six

Liturgy for Stressful Times

Lord, why does everything happen at once?
Why can't events be spaced out?
Why are commitments crowded in a few days
when next week the calendar is free?
Why do crises come when we're already booked?

The conference, ladies' tea, newsletter deadline,
monthly meeting, eye appointment,
out-of-town visitors, dinner guests,
as well as the last-minute wedding invitation,
urgent email, sudden funeral, early arrival,
broken fridge, twisted ankle, sick child.

I'm feeling anxious about getting it all done,
worried about forgetting something important,
afraid I'll make a mistake or double book,
perturbed because I have to say no to something,
irritated that I can't devote time to each one,
upset that I might have to declare the project
complete before it's perfect.

I confess I don't like being this busy,
rushing around or having to choose between great options.
I prefer to carefully schedule my events and commitments,
neatly organized with recovery time in between.

I admit I'm afraid of not performing perfectly,
I feel guilty for needing recoup time
and for not being as resilient as I'd like.
I confess that the busier I get,
the more I treat people as tasks to cross off my list
instead of as fellow image-bearers needing care.

I can't do it at all. What do I prioritize?
How do I know which one to let go?
Do I try to do everything now and make up for it later?

Lord Jesus, you were inundated with requests,
you didn't have time to debrief or even eat,
you tried to get away to a quiet place and rest
only to be followed and bombarded by more crowds
when you arrived at the "restful place."
So, you kept at it and fed 5,000,
you compassionately and miraculously met the need.
Only after all were fed did you retreat to pray.

You offered rest to your disciples too,
but their peaceful jaunt across the lake turned into a
harrowing fight for life in a ravaging storm.
You saw them, Lord, and you came walking on the water
to demonstrate your power and calm their fears.

Those moments with you in the boat, Lord, must've been sweet.
Fearful, yet witnessing your might and glory,
All together with you, their Savior.

Help me, Jesus, to capture moments alone with you
in the busyness, between events, amid the waves, on the boat.
Calm my storm, Lord, show your mighty power on my behalf,
multiply my meager efforts, give me courage to do the next thing
and compassion for those who need my help.

Even in the storm, even in the crowds, you are with me,
your greatness and power strengthen me to keep going.

Amen.[28]

31

Luxury vs. Hardship

God Gives Us What We Need

Your Father knows what you need before you ask him.
Matthew 6:8

I lived in a tropical island paradise. Yes, we had electricity outages regularly, mosquitoes, sweltering heat, and other annoyances. But we also enjoyed lush green vegetation, bougainvillea, frangipani, gardenia (my favorite), sunshine, white sand beaches, turquoise water, and delicious fruit like mangoes, papaya, and pineapple.

Though abounding in physical "fruit," I saw very little spiritual "fruit" from my labors. My husband, teammates, and local partners engaged in frequent spiritual conversations, but I rarely got into such discussions with local folks. I knew that God was at work in small ways. But there was no revival to report or even a small gathering of believers to write about as a direct result of my ministry. I never witnessed anyone turning to Christ.

Given this stark reality, I found comfort in the words of Isobel Kuhn, global messenger to China.[29] Kuhn first served Chinese farmers for ten years and saw very little spiritual fruit from her labors. Then she transitioned to continue the work begun by James Fraser among the *Lisu* people. Life carved out on the side of a mountain was difficult with no amenities or comforts and only basic food, but work among these people yielded an immense spiritual harvest. She speaks of this in her book, *In the Arena*,

> I needed the hard years of plodding, which resulted in little fruit, to make me so hungry for saved souls that the physical

> hardships would not matter. In other words, the Lord had to train me to appreciate what He was doing among that barefooted mountain tribe before He dared let me share in the work. I always said that Lisu work was physical hardship but spiritual luxury. The physical hardship was obvious to anyone. It was spiritual luxury I would not have recognized if I had gone right into Lisu work without those barren years among the Chinese peasants.[30]

I identified with Kuhn's contrast between hardship and luxury. For her, "Lisu work was physical hardship but spiritual luxury." For me, I deemed our work as spiritual hardship but our living conditions as physical luxury. Perhaps this was the mercy of God. I was grateful he gave lush surroundings to offset the barren spiritual landscape. He knew what I needed.

I believe God put me in that beautiful environment for a reason. When God asks his children to offer themselves as living sacrifices, they so often assume this means harsh living conditions and giving up amenities and conveniences. But instead, sacrificing for me meant getting out of my house, sharing the gospel more boldly with my acquaintances, even accompanying my husband to his work in the villages.

Kuhn helped me realize that whatever we face, God gives something to counterbalance it, some form of beauty in our labors for the Lord. For some, while they work in smelly surroundings, they enjoy the view of majestic mountains. For others, the demands on their attention may be endless, but privacy and a chance to get away can be found in a forest nearby. In the end, the "luxury" of our island life enabled me to endure the reality of seeing little spiritual fruit.

Read

Read Romans 5:3–5; Galatians 6:9; Hebrews 12:1; James 1:2–3, 12.
What do these verses tell you about God?
About your hardship or luxury?

Recount

Recall a time when God gave you a luxury to help you endure hardship. Who can you tell?

Respond

Thank you, Giver of all good things, for knowing what I need to endure. Give me eyes to look around and find the beauty when I don't see it right away. Help me to find the luxuries that offset the hardship. Teach me to rejoice in what you are doing, even if the evidence is elusive.

32

If It's You

Jesus Invites Us to Come to Him

"Lord, if it's you," Peter replied, "tell me to come to you on The water." "Come," he said. Then Peter got down out of the boat, walked on the water and came toward Jesus.
Matthew 14:28–29

During our first field conference, my husband and I took a few hours to enjoy some family time on a boat ride along the beautiful coastline. Our son was eighteen months old, and I was pregnant. The excursion was indeed relaxing and a feast for the eyes until we rounded a peninsula. The small craft began to rock vigorously, and the once gentle waves grew larger until they crashed onto the boat, spraying all of us passengers. Soon we shivered in our soaked clothing despite the warm sun and clear blue skies. The pleasant sightseeing jaunt had become a harrowing countdown until we reached shore. My poor husband, certain he had exposed his young family to mortal danger, was filled with relief when we finally disembarked (as was I).

Similarly, Jesus's disciples found themselves in a boat expecting to die (Matt. 14:22–33). Although experienced fishermen, they could not control their vessel. To make matters worse, a figure came toward them, walking on top of the water. They lost all composure, thinking it was a ghost. But Jesus identified himself and told them not to be afraid. Impulsive Peter then yelled out, "Lord, if it is you, tell me to come to you on the water" (Matt. 14:28).

Did he think about what he requested? Was he unfazed by

the huge waves? Did he want proof the shadowy figure was Jesus? Did he really have that much faith? Or perhaps he simply wanted to copy Jesus's amazing "trick."

Jesus replied, "Come," and Peter got out of the boat. He walked toward his rabbi. The text doesn't record how many steps he took, but at some point he noticed the strong wind and became afraid. He immediately started to sink. He cried out to Jesus for help and, of course, Jesus reached out his hand and saved him, saying, "Why did you doubt?" The passage ends with Jesus calming the winds and the disciples worshipping him as God.

I'd heard all the familiar lessons from this passage: *We need to take that first step of faith to get out of the boat. We sink when we take our eyes off Jesus and look at our circumstances. Don't doubt but have faith. Jesus, as the Son of God, has power over nature.*

But as a cross-cultural worker, it was Peter's words that I needed to apply: "Lord, *if it's you,* tell me to come to you" (emphasis mine). I faced big decisions and new opportunities to "step out of the boat," to use my gifts and skills. The needs seemed endless and my abilities small. I needed to attempt things I felt incapable of doing.

Did I genuinely hear my Savior's voice calling me, or was it yet another option? A legitimate need? Was I walking toward Jesus or to a semblance of him that seemed attractive? Could I even recognize my rabbi? I determined to pray and wait for him to identify himself first, so that I would know it was he who called me before I tried a new strategy or said yes to a task.

Once I had recognized the voice as truly his, then I asked him to tell me to come. I didn't want to step out or start walking until he had invited me to do so. I needed this assurance because the time might arise when he would ask me to "walk on water." And so, if I were sure Jesus had told me, "Come, have courage, do not be afraid," I could follow him. He would always reach out and catch me if I fell.

Read

Peruse Matthew 14:22–32; Mark 2:13–14; James 1:5–8.
What do these verses tell you about following God?
What big decision or uncertainty are you facing right now?

Recount

Remember a story about a time when you followed God's invitation to come to him and you stepped out in faith. Who can you share it with?

Respond

Jesus, my Savior, teach me to listen and to recognize your call. When you say so, I'll walk in faith toward your voice despite the difficult choices, hidden paths, or stormy circumstances.

33

Moped Accident

Jesus Helps Us Give Up Our Rights

> *Live such good lives among the pagans that, though they accuse you of doing wrong, they may see your good deeds and glorify God on the day he visits us.*
> 1 Peter 2:12

In the land of a million scooters, it was inevitable that we would collide with one at some point, as Mark did right outside our front gate one afternoon. When he stepped out of his car to check the damage, he stared in horror at a young woman lying on the ground with a disfigured leg. "Did I cause that?" he wondered.

A crowd gathered and began barking orders. Stunned, Mark transported the young woman and her driver to the hospital. There he learned that the disfigurement was actually due to polio, but the leg was broken and required surgery.

In this local culture, those with more means and the larger vehicle provided the funds for reparations. We felt compassion for her and wanted to display the love of Jesus. But in that context, it was complicated. And stressful.

A tough week followed. Mark slept fitfully, worrying about the accident and its consequences. (On top of this we were moving into our new home.) The day after the accident, the victim's father knocked on our door and handed us a receipt for a medical bill. He came again the next day. And the next, finally getting down on his knees and begging for us to take care of his daughter. In response, Mark begged him to stand. It was awkward and embarrassing for all of us.

Another day, the driver of the motorcycle appeared at the

house. Mark wasn't home, so I deferred her request for payment of the scooter repair, but the encounter left me shaken. The repair bill would be minor in comparison to the hospital bills, but we started to fear a never-ending chain of requests. Plus, we had little recourse to verify if the receipts were genuine.

The incessant requests for bill payments felt unfair. We wanted to face our obligation but not be taken advantage of. We wanted to live good lives that would glorify God yet not be manipulated into ongoing financial payments. Though we had auto insurance, we were advised that it was less bothersome to pay the victim than dealing with the insurance process. While we thought this may be an open door to share our faith, the interplay with money made it awkward at best.

We sought the advice of local friends. They prayed with us and instructed Mark in how to bring this process to a kind end. Following their advice, Mark tracked down the young girl's doctor and asked him to name the amount needed to cover her total expenses all the way to recovery.

Then Mark wrote up a "contract" stating he would give the family one lump sum to fulfill the obligation. The father could then pay the medical bills himself instead of stopping by for reimbursement of every receipt. Mark visited the father and presented him with the contract, they signed the arrangement, and Mark handed over the cash.

Once we got past the sting of the outgoing costs, we showed the family care by helping in other ways. We visited them in their home, bringing some food items. I took the opportunity to pray for the young woman in the name of Jesus.

The whole affair was tricky because we were the guests and benefactors. It felt unfair to be perceived as the one with endless funds, though comparatively, we were wealthy. We fought hard to not get angry, offended, closed-off, or cynical.

Through this experience, I was forced to admit I still had much to learn about my current cultural context. I perceived justice from an American perspective. I wanted the guilty party to pay. I wanted the situation to be handled fairly. But what did I know of injustice? The most this ordeal had cost us was money, time, irritation, and our perceived personal rights.

I asked the Lord to help me release my cultural bias. Rather than focusing on fairness, we could own our part and make restitution where possible. Then I could focus on Jesus's commands to "Do good to those who hate you . . . pray for those who mistreat you . . . if anyone takes what belongs to you, do not demand it back. Do to others as you would have them do to you . . . lend to them without expecting to get anything back . . . Be merciful, just as your Father is merciful" (Luke 6:27–36).

Read

Meditate on Luke 6:27–36.
What is Jesus saying to you through these verses?

Recount

Recount a time when God helped you lay aside your own cultural concept of justice to respond as Jesus would.

Respond

Lord Jesus, it can be hard to take responsibility for my own mistakes, and it doesn't feel nice to be manipulated. Help me to walk the tension between letting go of my own cultural sense of justice and walking wisely and kindly, allowing you to work in the situation. Teach me how to simply love and serve so that others will see you and glorify you (1 Pet. 2:12).

34

Home Assignment

God is Worth Celebrating

They celebrate your abundant goodness and
joyfully sing of your righteousness.
Psalm 145:7

The Indonesian language has a unique phrase, *mau, tidak mau.* It literally means "want, don't want." This ditty perfectly described my complicated relationship with home assignment (or furlough as we called it when I was young)—that interruption of life and routine, yet a necessary connection with family and churches. I wanted, yet at the same time didn't want, to return to the U.S.

On the one hand, the Great Commission is a joint venture with our partners and donors, and they deserve in-person updates. I was excited by the prospect of seeing loved ones again, functioning in English, and enjoying familiar conveniences and amenities. I looked forward to being away from the craziness of life on the island.

Yet on the other hand, the U.S. still wasn't home to me. Residue from my life as a TCK cropped up every time I returned. The readjustment to American culture often made me feel dumb and stupid like I had felt as a child. On top of this, furlough brought back memories of extended travel, visiting strangers, reciting my parents' presentation by heart, and being "on show" in front of church congregations. It meant transition, suitcases, strange beds, and lack of routine.

On one furlough, I wrote in my journal:

> Some of my childhood feelings have returned: feeling overwhelmed in large stores, the smell of the cool, dry air, fear of driving in the driver's seat, wondering if people think I'm weird.

If I still felt this way about home assignment as a grown adult, how was I going to help my own children maneuver it? I was sensitive to their goodbyes and the friends they missed even as they were excited to see grandparents and cousins. I worried about their adjustment to a local American school.

During our first furlough my youngest son perfectly echoed my own feelings: "Mommy, why do we go to someone else's house every day to eat?" Another day during lunch in someone else's home, he genuinely wanted to know, "Why are we here, Mom?"

The Lord began to help me reframe my view of home assignment from a time of "reporting" to one of "refreshing." If I sought to encourage, affirm, and challenge others, I would, in turn, be refreshed (Prov. 11:25). This helped give purpose to our frequent one-on-one interactions.

Mark and I also asked the Lord to give us another way to view our public presentations. We didn't want to make it all about the crises we had experienced. I was also feeling some uncertainty about speaking publicly, not wanting to flaunt myself or assume that I should have a hearing based on my unique overseas experiences. But I did feel some excitement about the possibility of sharing truth from Scripture that I had learned while overseas and giving glory to God for all he had done.

God answered our request. He gave my husband the idea of leading a worship service based on the past years. That excited me too. We put together a celebration of God's faithfulness based on Lamentations 3:22–24, complete with verses, songs, and testimonies of what God had done. We would simply adapt the presentation to the audience and allotted time.

Anytime we were given more than a few minutes to share, we recounted the goodness of God to us and our team during the previous years. This way, the service did not focus on us or what we had encountered, but rather, about God and what he had done. This format worked wonderfully and totally reframed my view of home assignment.

Read

Check out Acts 14:27–28; Philippians 1:3–5; 1 Thessalonians 3:10–11; 2 John 1:12.
What is God saying to you through these verses?

Recount

Remember when God helped you celebrate his faithfulness with your family or partners. How might you recreate this celebration?

Respond

Great God, I am grateful for your enabling to face the changes in lifestyle, culture, and ministry interruption that accompanied home assignment. Help global messengers not see it as only reporting but as a chance to celebrate your faithfulness with their partners, family, and friends. May we all be refreshed as we seek to minister and refresh others.

35

Unproductive

Jesus Helps Us Do the Next Thing

All these people were still living by faith when they died. They did not receive the things promised; they only saw them and welcomed them from a distance, admitting that they were foreigners and strangers on earth.
Hebrews 11:13

I attempted to visit my local friend, Nella, but it wasn't convenient for her. I tried to take some sewing to a tailor but was told it would be a month before it would be ready. I could sew it myself in less time. Then I delivered some film to be developed (before the days of digital cameras), only to discover when I arrived at the photo store that I had left it at home. I wanted to submit our sons' application forms to the new school, but they weren't ready with the cost estimates and bank numbers, so I had to wait another few days. The propane tank for our gas stove was leaking again and wouldn't be replaced until the next day. And the car alarm didn't work. Who knew when that would be fixed?

Days like this were common and seemingly pointless. And I didn't like feeling unproductive. I preferred to cross things off my to-do list, to get tasks done. I used tear-off note pads and made lists and lists of what needed to be done each day and the next. I included undesirable yet necessary tasks as well as life-giving ones. When each item was completed, I drew a line through the words. Done. Finished. Wrapped up. Nice and neat. And I tossed the list in the trash. While some people prefer the process of doing a task, I found most delight in the completion of it. Only then did I feel productive. Only then could I sit down and rest.

The problem with my system was that so many of my lists remained "in process." Rarely did I ever get to the end of any list. On most days, a few items got carried over to a new list when the old paper was full. And because stuff was never totally done, I lived in limbo.

As I tried to unearth the unrest in my soul, I realized that I was believing the myth that I could not live contentedly unless I was productive. I turned to the examples in the Bible's "Hall of Faith" in Hebrews 11. They "were still living by faith when they died. They did not receive the things promised" (Heb. 11:13).

Their very lives seemed unfinished. So how could I reframe my own unsettledness? I kept reading in Hebrews.

> Therefore, since we are surrounded by such a great cloud of witnesses, let us throw off everything that hinders and the sin that so easily entangles. And let us run with perseverance the race marked out for us, fixing our eyes on Jesus, the pioneer and perfecter of faith. For the joy set before him he endured the cross, scorning its shame, and sat down at the right hand of the throne of God. Consider him who endured such opposition from sinners, so that you will not grow weary and lose heart. (Heb. 12:1–3)

My mother often told me to just "do the next thing." I think she learned this from Elisabeth Elliot who got it from an old Saxon legend:

> Do it immediately, do it with prayer; Do it reliantly, casting all care; Do it with reverence, tracing His hand Who placed it before thee with earnest command. Stayed on Omnipotence, safe 'neath His wing, Leave all results, do the next thing.[31]

It was enough to go home and do the next thing, whether it was laundry, or supper, or putting the boys to bed. I had to offer up my lack of results or productivity to God. He knew I had tried. He knew all about the circumstances and the interruptions and delays. I was the impatient one, the frustrated one.

I could plug away, focusing on Jesus and not on my lists or perceived productivity. I could contemplate his sacrifice and endurance to help me not grow weary and give up. I could remember that true rest is found in Jesus and not in a completed list.

Read

Meditate on Hebrews 12:1–3.
How does Jesus's example encourage you today?

Recount

Recall a time when God helped you just do the next thing when feeling unproductive. Who can you tell?

Respond

Jesus, my Savior, thank you that you endured with joy so that I can know true rest in you. I don't need to strive to accomplish my tasks to gain approval from you or contentment for my soul. Teach me to endure in the daily mundane, to do the next thing, and to look with faith toward you.

36

Ultimate Date

God Empowers Us to Stand Firm

Therefore, my dear brothers and sisters, stand firm.
Let nothing move you. Always give yourselves
fully to the work of the Lord, because you know
that your labor in the Lord is not in vain.
1 Corinthians 15:58

Sometimes my husband and I just had to get away to indulge in some comforts. So, when we heard that our favorite story had finally become a major motion picture, we made plans to see it. This meant choosing a free day in the schedule, finding babysitters for our boys (thank you, dear teammates), and booking flights to the neighboring island.

Yes, we actually flew one hundred miles to see *The Fellowship of the Ring*. A day away from work and responsibility comprised the ultimate destination date. We enjoyed eating out, shopping, and of course, losing ourselves in the drama of Middle Earth and the nine heroes who pledged to save the world by destroying the ring of power.

We gazed in amazement at the special effects and beauty of the film, while I mentally compared it to the book (I am a Tolkien fan after all). But one scene involving the group's leader, Aragorn, vividly stood out to me. It both illustrated the spiritual battle we waged daily and offered a strategy to follow, one rooted in Scripture.

During their journey, the nine warriors are chased by orcs (evil creatures) who finally catch up to them, determined to seize the ring. When Aragorn realizes the enemy is upon them, he orders the ring-bearer (Frodo) to flee. Then he turns—all alone since his fellow warriors are dealing with the enemy on other fronts—to face the advancing army. He is grossly outnumbered, yet he does not run away or even flinch. Rather, he stands his ground, draws his sword, and begins fighting madly. This lone hero, representing the side of goodness and truth, stands firm.

We are told to "stand firm" many times in Scripture. This phrase intrigued me, and I wanted to understand and practice it. I believed this principle would help us as we attempted to shine the light of Jesus in the dark place where we lived and served. I searched for other examples of "standing firm."

When the Israelites were chased by the Egyptians to the Red Sea, Moses told them to stand firm (Exod. 14:13). When facing the Moabites and Ammonites, Jehoshaphat told the people, "Take up your positions; stand firm and see the deliverance the LORD will give you . . . Do not be afraid; do not be discouraged. Go out to face them tomorrow, and the LORD will be with you" (2 Chron. 20:17). The apostle Paul instructed believers to "Be on your guard; stand firm in the faith; be courageous; be strong" (1 Cor. 16:13). And of course, I cannot forget the most well-known admonition, "Stand firm then, with the belt of truth buckled around your waist" (Eph. 6:14).

According to the Topical Encyclopedia, "Standing firm is a biblical concept that refers to maintaining one's faith, convictions, and moral integrity in the face of challenges, temptations, or opposition. It is a call to steadfastness and perseverance, rooted in the strength and guidance provided by God."[32]

I then found some clues about how to do this:

> We [who trust in the Lord] will rise up and stand firm. (Ps. 20:8)

> It is God who makes both of us and you stand firm in Christ. (2 Cor. 1:21)

> It is by faith you stand firm. (2 Cor. 1:24)

> Resist the devil, standing firm in the faith because brothers throughout the world are undergoing the same kind of struggle. (1 Pet. 5:9)

If I were to successfully stand firm in the face of opposition or trial like Aragorn modeled in the movie, then I would not run away despite the size of the opposition. Instead, I would trust in the name of God and maintain my position faithfully.

Read

Look up and meditate on any of the verses referenced above. What do they tell you about the trial you are facing?

Recount

Describe a time when God empowered you to stand firm. Who might need your encouragement to persevere?

Respond

King of Glory, teach me to conduct myself in a manner worthy of the gospel of Christ. Then I will stand firm in your spirit, contending for the gospel, without being frightened by those who oppose me (Phil. 1:27–28). Help me to stand firm in all the will of God, mature and fully assured (Col. 4:12).

Week Seven

Liturgy for Increasing Faith

Lord, my responsibilities are growing.
You've asked me to mentor these women,
lead them in Bible study, and
encourage their spiritual growth.

I feel overwhelmed most of the time,
like I don't know what I'm doing.

I sense that you're testing me
as you did the disciples
when you saw the great crowd approaching.
You asked where they could buy bread to feed everyone.

You asked even though you had a plan all along.
You already knew what you were going to do.

Likewise, I sense you're asking me
how I'm going to "feed"
all these you're sending my way.

And like Philip, I answer
"It will take more resources, more time,
and more talent than I have, Lord."

Or like Andrew, "I offer my talent, such as it is,
and limited resources,
but I don't see how that's going to help
when the needs are so great."

Remind me, Lord, that you took the five loaves
and two fish and multiplied them,
enough for all to be fed
with more to spare.

You already knew what you were going to do.

Likewise, you already know how to feed these women.
Lord, increase my tiny faith.

And then you withdrew by yourself to pray.
But that's another lesson for another day.

Amen.[33]

37

What Spills Out

God Produces Good Fruit in Us

A good man brings good things out of the good stored up in his heart, and an evil man brings evil things out of the evil stored up in his heart. For the mouth speaks what the heart is full of.
Luke 6:45

As a member of another agency, Anna had no team of her own, so she partnered with ours. We fully embraced this vivacious, witty woman who so exuded love for Jesus.

One day she rose early since she was hosting a guest—another potential worker. She had planned a full day of sightseeing and an overview of the local ministry. Anna's daily routine began with a cup of tea, so she entered her small kitchen to heat water. As she applied flame to the gas stove, her day came to an abrupt halt. The gas line had leaked, and she was engulfed in flames.

Hearing Anna's cry, her guest ran to her aid. She immediately grabbed a blanket to smother the flames, then called a teammate. Word spread, and others soon arrived to drive Anna to the local hospital. Two of our co-workers, one with critical care nursing experience, began to look after her at the hospital (local nurses and doctors left them alone) as others began the laborious process of initiating a medical evacuation from the island to her home in Singapore.

Anna knew the risks of living in a foreign place. Once she wrote to her supervisor:

> I am not against caution, but safety and common sense is NOT necessarily God's will and best for me. God's sovereignty and plans are NOT always common sense and rational. I REALISE (sic) more deeply than ever before that life and death is really in God's hand. We are All going to die one day.[34]

While we waited all day for the medical airplane, we took turns sitting by Anna's bed, praying with her, and distracting her from the excruciating pain. Miraculously she remained stable—conscious and lucid and able to bear the pain with only oral medication and small tubes of topical ointment. And prayer. When Anna expressed that the pain grew overwhelming, we called on the Lord, and he eased her torment. In response she murmured, "Jesus Christ is enough. He is enough for me." She also spoke of her desire to return after treatment to finish the work she'd begun.

As I prayed with Anna, I recalled that she had recently shared her desire to be changed from the inside out.

"When a pail is kicked over," she'd said, "its contents spill out. I want to live in such a way that forgiveness, love, gentleness, and kindness pour out whenever I am beaten down—not bitterness, hurt, unforgiveness, and self-defensiveness."

Twelve hours after the accident, the medevac plane arrived and transported Anna to an intensive care unit in her home country. Doctors confirmed that the burns covered 85 percent of her body, the worst on her chest and upper arms. For the next three weeks, she received several skin grafts, but the infection raged and entered her lungs. Her breathing slowed. She finally entered into Jesus's presence where she felt no more pain, suffering, uncertain future, nor the troubles of ministry.

God answered Anna's request. When she was beaten down, we witnessed her kind and gentle spirit. Her earthly "pail" had been destroyed, but the contents—the true Anna—spilled out in triumph and perfect love.

Read

Read Proverbs 4:23; Psalm 51:10; 1 Samuel 16:7; Matthew 12:33–35; Mark 7:20–23.
What do these verses tell you about God's perspective on the contents of our heart?

Recount

Recall and tell a friend about a time when you were kicked and beaten down and yet God helped you display "good fruit."

Respond

Holy Spirit, thank you for Anna's beauty that overflowed even during severe pain. I fear I could never endure something as terrible as a physical burning, but I trust you will enable me to face whatever tragedy comes my way. Keep developing your fruit in me, so that when I am kicked over, the inside beauty of forgiveness, love, gentleness, and kindness will flow out.

38

A Tribute to Anna

God Commends Us for Our Faith

These were all commended for their faith, yet none of them received what had been promised. God had planned something better for us so that only together with us would they be made perfect.
Hebrews 11:39–40

The last time our teammate, Anna, worshipped with us, she asked prayer for three things. First, she desired her speech to be gentler. Second, for a greater heart for evangelism. And third, for the chance to share the gospel with her mother.

God answered her first request. During her memorial services, her friends testified of Anna's timely advice and wisdom. Some mentioned that she was forthright at times but never too harsh or rough. It was evident that God had used her words to advise many.

I believe God answered her second request. Proclaiming her faith in our location carried an added danger because she was a Chinese Singaporean. But she knew it was God's place for her. She demonstrated her commitment to sharing the gospel despite the risks when she stayed in country during the riots and encouraged her national co-laborers to continue testifying even as they feared further persecution.

She told them, "I could die here. I'm going to die sometime no matter where I am. I could die sitting in a chair in Singapore drinking Coke or watching TV. But I'd rather die here doing something meaningful and purposeful with my life." For Anna, that purpose was testifying of new life in Christ.

Her frequent challenge stuck with me: "Hello, what are you doing? You're not dead yet! You're still alive! Get out there and tell people there is hope and salvation in Jesus."

Regarding her third request, Anna did not see her mother come to faith before she died. But many of her friends shared the gospel with her mother during the three weeks that Anna lay in the hospital fighting for her life. Anna's mother heard many stories about her daughter, how the translation was more than just a project, how it was Anna's desire to see the Word of God penetrate and change the lives of the translators themselves. Her mother heard about how Anna saw their needs, understood their moods and encouraged them, and how she had a timely piece of advice or counsel on each occasion.

I think Anna deserves a place in Hebrews 11 along with the other great men and women of faith. The author makes two lists of unnamed persons.

The first group were the ones who:

> Through faith conquered kingdoms, administered justice, and gained what was promised; who shut the mouths of lions, quenched the fury of the flames, and escaped the edge of the sword; whose weakness was turned to strength; and who became powerful in battle and routed foreign armies. Women received back their dead, raised to life again. (Heb. 11:33–35)

The second group were not so fortunate:

> There were others who were tortured, refusing to be released so that they might gain an even better resurrection. Some faced jeers and flogging, and even chains and imprisonment. They were put to death by stoning; they were sawed in two; they were killed by the sword. They went about in sheepskins and goatskins, destitute, persecuted and mistreated—the world was not worthy of them. They wandered in deserts and mountains, living in caves and in holes in the ground. (Heb. 11:35–38)

The writer concludes by saying, "These were all commended for their faith" (Heb. 11:39). *All of them*—those in the first group who experienced obvious victory as well as those in the second who suffered apparent defeat. In other words, God's recognition of our faith does not depend on what we (or others) consider to be a "successful" outcome.

Anna didn't get to choose which of these two groups she joined. Her responsibility was only to exercise faith. She did that. Marvelously. Even though Anna did not live to see the results of her efforts or prayer requests, she is commended for her faith.

Read

Check out 1 Corinthians 12:8–11; 2 Corinthians 4:18; Galatians 5:22; Hebrews 11:1.
What does God say about your faith?

Recount

Remember a time when you felt that God commended you for your faith. Who can you tell?

Respond

Yahweh, there are many things for which I have asked you and have yet to see the answers. Help me to have faith like Anna, to believe that, despite what I may experience in life, all that I have asked for you to accomplish through my life will one day come to pass.

39

Receding Supply

God Provides Finances

> *The ravens brought [Elijah] bread and meat in the morning and bread and meat in the evening, and he drank from the brook. Some time later the brook dried up because there had been no rain in the land.*
> *1 Kings 17:6–8*

Each month when my husband read our financial statement, he commented in amazement, "Bless these dear people. They're still giving to us." We relied on financial gifts from donors and partners for our ministry and personal needs. Actually, we still do.

But one month Mark opened the report and noted a significant lack of funds. We had received less than anticipated, and we were alarmed. Caught off guard and fearful, we put a moratorium on spending. We made lists of what we needed to do and not do to make up for the deficit.

We had experienced the faithful and abundant provision of the Lord only to see it threaten to dry up. A bit like Elijah. Even though famine had come to the land God provided for Elijah, a brook supplied his need for water, and ravens brought him bread and meat twice a day.

Yet this supply wasn't endless. At some point (days, weeks, months?) the brook dried up. Did Elijah's worry increase as he saw the brook recede lower and lower? Did he stress out about where his next drink would come from? I know I would have.

The narrative states that God then directed Elijah to his next provision—a widow with a handful of flour and a little bit of oil. At first glance, her contribution hardly qualified as sustenance. It seemed unjust for Elijah to consume the wee bit that she had left, enough only for one meal for herself and her son. But God had promised, and so the flour and oil remained constant until the famine was over (1 Kings 17:14; 18:1).

How quickly I forgot God's provision for us just a few years earlier, prior to our departure to Indonesia. As that deadline loomed, we still lacked adequate monthly support to leave, and we cried out to the Lord in desperation. In reply, God filled my husband with a calm assurance that he was going to provide. But I wanted the security of specific pledges and amounts so that we could know the exact number of dollars coming in each month. In retrospect, what kind of faith did I possess?

At that time a dear friend called to see how I was doing. When I shared my struggle, she calmly reminded me of countless servants of God who pioneered in foreign lands before us. Where was their list of monthly supporters? Did they ever really know how much money they could live off each month? I felt a burden lift as I listened to her words. Yes, God would provide. I vowed to no longer look to our monthly supporter list as my security. Instead, I trusted the Lord to supply our financial needs each month.

And yet, here I was, years later, doubting again as the water in the proverbial brook receded ever lower. We prayed and reminded ourselves that God had not yet left us "begging for bread" (Ps. 37:25). An ebbing brook wasn't a sign of God's abandonment. Author Melissa Spoelstra in her Bible study on Elijah puts it into perspective,

> Sometimes following God means standing alone and waiting while the brook we are drinking from goes dry, but we can trust God to take care of us. As we see Him continually show His faithfulness in our lives, we develop spiritual stamina that enables us to "freak out" less and trust Him more![35]

We were hardly starving and could still pay our bills. Our reaction proved greater than the actual crisis. God had always been our provider, and he would continue to be so.

Read

Peruse 1 Kings 17:1–16; Psalm 37:23–27; Philippians 4:15–20. How do these verses help you trust God for financial provision?

Recount

Think back to when God provided for your financial needs. Who can you tell about God's faithful care?

Respond

Jehovah Jireh, how quickly I forget that you provided all the financial provision we needed all the years we served overseas and beyond. Now, when things are a bit lean, help me trust you anew. Teach me to release my doubts again and again, for you will not let me or my children beg for bread.

40

Post 9/11

God Calms Our Fear of Bad News

They will have no fear of bad news; their hearts are steadfast, trusting in the Lord. Their hearts are secure, they will have no fear; in the end they will look in triumph on their foes.
Psalm 112:7–8

After the attacks on the World Trade Center and the Pentagon on September 11, 2001, our corner of the world speculated what might happen if the U.S. attacked Afghanistan. A radical Muslim group began passing out leaflets asking for the removal of U.S. citizens from the island, and, while they were at it, all the Christians. I felt the familiar grip of fear on my heart as I drove around town. *Should I hide the fact that I am American? Are we really going to go through this again?*

Mark and I prayed for leaders and grieving families in the U.S. while rejoicing that nothing drastic immediately happened on the island. Just in case, we repacked our evacuation bag and made arrangements for a potential quick departure. Previous experience made us both weary and wary of reacting without preparation and caution. We prayed to act wisely.

We also prayed for our boys. They were the only Americans in their school, and the teachers kept us informed of any threats. The school gates were locked during hours of instruction. The boys appeared fine (as far as I could tell) and oblivious to world events. I asked God to help us all face whatever evil we might encounter, believing that he would enable us to bear it.

I attempted to concentrate on tasks at hand yet wondered

how much more time I would have to enjoy life as I had come to know it. I continued to meet with the ladies on the national team. We studied God's attributes. As I got to know his character, I found I could trust him more. I especially clung to his greatness. The enemy I saw around me in the world was not bigger than my mighty God (1 John 4:4). The kings and leaders were in his hands (Prov. 21:1). My days on earth were decided by him, not by world events (Ps. 139:16).

Therefore, I could trust that his plans were good even if they included some trauma and loss (Jer. 29:11–13). I could be strong and endure hardship (2 Tim. 2:1–3). Even though things were far from peaceful outside, I could experience peace inside (John 16:33). And most significantly, I did not need to live in dread of the next crisis (Prov. 3:25–26). If my heart was steadfast and trusting in the Lord, I would have no fear of bad news (Ps. 112:7–8). I did not want to let the uncertainty of the future bring anxiety in the present. This day's problems were enough for today (Matt. 6:34). As I had during the riots, I surrendered the potential of leaving the home that I knew and loved. And I increased my resolve to share the message of the gospel.

Rather than bad news, we instead received some good news. My parents invited us to visit them in Papua New Guinea to attend the dedication of the *Saposa* New Testament that they had helped translate. Witnessing God's faithfulness to my parents enlarged my steadfast heart to entrust any future "bad news" to God.

Read

Look up and meditate on the verses above.
How can you trust God with a steadfast, secure heart?

Recount

Describe a time when God calmed your fear of some bad news. How might you preserve this story for the next generation?

Respond

O Lord my God, I sometimes fear that another crisis will come or that an email or phone call will bring yet more bad news. You tell me that my heart can be steadfast, trusting in you. Teach me to keep living in your security and not in dread of another crisis.

41

Victoria Falls

God Loves Us Lavishly

See what great love the Father has lavished on us, that we should be called children of God! And that is what we are!
1 John 3:1

When ministry intensified and tension between teammates grew, I needed to learn how to love more fully and effectively. I embarked on a thorough study of love.

The New Testament word for love is *agape*. *Agape* originates with God (1 John 4:7), for God himself *is* love (1 John 4:8). He loved us first (1 John 4:19) and demonstrated love to us:

> This is how God showed his love among us: He sent his one and only Son into the world that we might live through him. This is love: not that we loved God, but that he loved us and sent his Son as an atoning sacrifice for our sins. (1 John 4:9–10)

My favorite adjective for God's love is "lavish" (1 John 3:1). Lavish makes me think of a rainfall shower head that dispenses water profusely. Liberally, abundantly, extravagantly. Without holding anything back.

I searched for every reference to love in Scripture. I saturated my mind and heart with the truth that I was loved lavishly. I did this so that my soul would be filled with God and his love, so that I would run to him, and not to my teammates, for my fulfillment and validation.

Having drunk from the bountiful supply of God's love, I could then focus on Jesus's new command, "Love each other as I have loved you" (John 15:12; 13:34). Since God filled me up lavishly with his love, I had extra to overflow to others. The apostle John repeats this theme over and over.

> We should love one another. (1 John 3:11)
>
> We ought to lay down our lives for our brothers and sisters. (1 John 3:16)
>
> Let us not love with words or tongue but with actions and in truth. (1 John 3:18)
>
> Let us love one another. (1 John 4:7)
>
> Since God so loved us, we also ought to love one another. (1 John 4:11)
>
> Whoever loves God must also love her brother and sister. (1 John 4:21)

I experienced an illustration of this lavish love during one of our trips back to the U.S. En route, we took the opportunity to visit my brother and his family in Africa, where they served as cross-cultural workers. The highlight of our trip was a day at Victoria Falls—the world's longest waterfall. This natural wonder spans one mile across the border of Zimbabwe and Zambia and drops 420 feet into the gorge below.

Imagine our amazement and awe at God's handiwork as we walked along the opposite ridge, viewing the falls from many angles, and feeling the spray of 550,000 cubic meters of water falling every minute. It was a lavish display of grandeur I will never forget.

Soon after we started our home assignment, a friend took my husband and ten-year-old son camping in Ohiopyle State Park in western Pennsylvania. While there, they stopped to view Ohiopyle Falls, a mere twenty-foot drop.

My young son was not impressed at all. He took one look, turned to his dad and said, "This is so not . . . not . . . not . . . not . . . not . . . Victoria Falls." After experiencing the lavish display of Victoria Falls, he was no longer moved by what seemed a mere trickle.

God wanted to lavish his love on me like Victoria Falls. He didn't want me to be satisfied with a trickle. As I basked in his lavish love, I had enough to satisfy my needs with an abundant overflow for my teammates.

Read

Skim the whole book of 1 John.
What is God saying to you about his love?

Recount

Recount a time when you experienced God's lavish love that also overflowed to others.

Respond

Loving Savior, I run to you today, asking you to pour your lavish love into my parched heart. Satisfy all the hollow places with your unfailing love. Forgive me for being satisfied with a mere trickle of love. Free me from craving the approval of others or requiring them to fill my emotional cup. Give me so much of your love that it overflows to those around me. Teach me how to love like you do—putting others' needs before my own, serving, and showing love with actions.

42

More Valuable

God Brings Help in Time of Need

Are not five sparrows sold for two pennies?
Yet not one of them is forgotten by God.
Indeed, the very hairs of your head are all numbered.
Don't be afraid; you are worth more than many sparrows.
Luke 12:6–7

We met Nella soon after we arrived in country. She taught Sunday school for our boys at the church we began attending. We loved her immediately. Her childlike faith often encouraged and challenged me.

Nella was born into a Christian family on an eastern island. She accepted Christ as her Savior at an evangelistic service when she was a teenager. After high school, she heard about an opportunity to go to Bible school, so she set off without parental permission or money. God saw her need and supplied a global worker to support her through school. From the outset of her spiritual journey, Nella trusted in God for her complete financial and material provision and experienced his help in amazing ways.

Being single, she lived alone although this was uncommon in her society. Because she had no partner or roommate, little problems like leaky faucets and locked doors became insurmountable difficulties. One day, Nella found herself with more than a leaky faucet—she had a flood. For a full day, the water ran. On the evening of the second day, after trying various stop-gap measures, she plugged her ears, prayed that God would stop the flow, and went to sleep.

In the morning, the water had not let up. So, she set out to find a serviceman. But that day was a national holiday, and no one was working. She returned home, discouraged. Things only got worse. As she approached her home she discovered she had lost her house keys.

With no other recourse, she broke into her home through a window. First, she sat right down and prayed, "Lord, please send a repairman to fix my faucet and please bring my keys back." Then she mopped up the floor and dried out boxes of wet books.

That afternoon, she noticed a man wandering up and down her street. It turned out that he was looking for her house. When he found it, Nella discovered he was a plumber. He fixed the faucet in no time. I forget if Nella ever told me how the man knew to come to her home. Perhaps her inquiries the day before had reached his ears. Either way, God miraculously answered her plea for help.

The next day during the ride home from church, a woman handed her some keys, saying, "You dropped these yesterday as you departed." In a city with thousands of mini-buses that transport millions of people every day, Nella ended up with the same woman who had picked up her keys the day before. Another miracle!

"I know God takes care of me," Nella shared with me, "I have experienced firsthand that I am way more valuable than a whole flock of sparrows."

Read

Open your Bible to Matthew 6:25–34; 12:11–12.
How can you know you are infinitely valuable to God?

Recount

Tell someone about a time when God showed how valuable you were by bringing help when you needed it.

Respond

Eternal God, thank you for knowing all the intimate details of my life. I don't always feel valuable, so help me believe your Word which tells me I am more valuable than a whole flock of birds. Show me how much you care for me, and provide for all my needs.

Week Eight

Liturgy After Intense Ministry

Lord God, I'm so weary.
I feel like I could cry but I'm not sure what about.
I've run a sprint and I need to pause, rest, reset.

I think it was successful.
With your help I reached my goals.
I served, taught, empathized, encouraged,
adapted, pivoted, listened,
prayed incessantly, and survived.

You enabled me to serve well,
to make recommendations, share resources
and give the gift of presence.
And I am grateful.

On this side I'm tired and depleted.
And I must regroup to keep going.

I can only do so much,
I cannot carry all their burdens,
cannot make others change
(that's your job, Lord).

So, I give them to you, Jesus, I let them go.
For now, I "file away" their stuff.
I ask you to take them from my crowded heart
and look after them.

I release these dear ones into your care.
Holy Spirit, speak to them, teach,
counsel, and pursue them.
Where I proved inadequate and my counsel feeble,
fill them up with your truth,
remove anything I said that wasn't helpful.

LITURGY AFTER INTENSE MINISTRY

As you continue to minister to those I ministered to,
minister to me as well.
I meet with you in quiet solitude
and strengthen myself in you.
I release the burdens shared with me
to you, my ultimate burden bearer,
consummate counselor,
advocate and comforter.

Replenish my soul, strengthen my body,
pour life and joy into my heart.
May my life-giving activities truly restore,
my recreation truly re-create,
my sleep truly refresh.

You promise to give energy to those
who are tired and worn out,
you say that I will wake refreshed from my sleep.
I call on you and you answer me,
you increase my strength of soul.
I rely on your mighty power.

I ask that I might do the next thing—
in your power, by your strength,
with a full heart,
eager to serve and minister once again.

Amen.[36]

43

The "M" Word

God Gives Insight to Navigate Identity

This is why I speak to them in parables: "Though seeing, they do not see; though hearing, they do not hear or understand."
Matthew 13:13

"Mom, I know what the 'm' word is," my son declared from the back seat of our car. My husband and I looked at each other with a little concern. *Oh no, this is it,* I thought. We had managed to keep it under wraps for eight years. Now, we'd have to do some explaining.

Due to the sensitive nature of our work, we never referred to ourselves as mi**aries. We entered the country on work visas, and therefore my husband taught English or researched music. Among our colleagues, we referred to ourselves as "M's." (During the past decade, we've adopted other labels such as "cross-cultural worker" or "global messenger.") The fact that our son had figured it out was not really a surprise. He was bound to sooner or later.

Like many other children, our son encountered swear words by accident on a public playground. Just learning to read, he sounded out some letters scratched into the metal of a swing and proudly intoned, "f***." Liking the sound the letters made, he skipped around the playground repeating his newly discovered word.

When my husband caught up with him, a quick lesson in forbidden words followed. Over time, he also discovered the "s" and the "d" word. Thus, his curiosity with the "m" word.

"What is the "m" word?" his father asked him cautiously.

"Moron!" he proudly proclaimed.

We burst out laughing. "Yes, you're right, it is not nice to call someone a moron." Relief. Our secret was safe, and considering ourselves and our colleagues, he wasn't too far off.

This humorous experience illustrated one of our daily tensions. How should we answer questions posed to us about our reason for moving to and living in this country? We sought to obey God's command, "Do not lie" (Col. 3:9), and American culture pressured us to "Tell the truth, the whole truth, and nothing but the truth." Yet we served in a country where proselytizing was illegal, and our work visa did not reflect the underlying purpose for our presence in that society.

I turned to some examples in the Bible for insight into this dilemma.

Two Hebrew midwives, Shiphrah and Puah lied (or did not tell the whole truth) to Pharaoh when he questioned why they had not killed the baby boys as ordered (Exod. 1:15–19). Whatever the facts around the birthing experiences of Hebrew women, God did not call the midwives out for their words. Instead, he commended them for fearing and obeying him.

Samuel received God's command to anoint a new king. He obeyed but did not disclose the real intent of that mission (i.e. the whole truth). He fulfilled his promise by offering a sacrifice but secretly anointed a new king (David) in the process (1 Sam. 16:1–5).

Joshua sent his spies into Jericho. They sought the help of Rahab, an innkeeper, who hid them on her roof. When the king's messengers came looking for the spies, Rahab misled them. For this deceit, she was not punished. Rather, God saved her because of her faith in him (Josh. 2:1–24; Heb. 11:31).

Jesus himself did not answer questions directly. He replied with a question of his own, remained silent, or redirected the conversation back to others. He taught in parables to reveal, as well as conceal, the truth from people (Matt. 13:10–17). And while doing so, he lived a life without sin.

From these examples, I gleaned that God did not condemn me if I withheld certain details of my identity and purpose. Rather, he rewarded faith and obedience above all. When confronted, I could answer vaguely and refrain from offering extra unrequested information. And in a tight spot, the Holy Spirit would teach me what to say (Luke 12:11–12).

We took one day at a time and prayerfully tried to do our best to answer queries truthfully without divulging more than necessary. My husband worked within the terms of his visa. We identified ourselves as Jesus followers (Luke 9:23–27). We didn't allow fear of deportation to keep us from developing relationships or sharing our faith as we had opportunity. We guarded our endeavors so that we would not cause harm to the local believers with whom we partnered.

Read

Look up the verses referenced and meditate on them.
What insight do they offer about navigating the tension between telling the whole truth and protecting yourself?

Recount

Record a story about a time when God gave you wisdom to know how to describe your work and why you do it.

Respond

Wise God, we want to be brave servants of yours, but we also want we serve. Thank you for not condemning us when we withhold details of our identity. And thank you that being your child is our true identity.

44

Provoked

God Enables Us to Spur Others On

And let us consider how we may spur one another on to love and good deeds.
Hebrews 10:24

"Why don't you take over the women's Bible study? Come along with me to a village to share your testimony. I'm planning a retreat for the local church planters' wives, and you can share the devotions."

My teammate's many suggestions for serving sometimes provoked me. I was a young and tentative cross-cultural worker. I didn't feel ready. I didn't have her extroverted evangelistic gift. It was easier to stay at home and remain within my safe, comfortable haven. But she believed in me and continued to create opportunities for me—all the while cheering for me. She "spurred me on" as the anonymous author of Hebrews teaches us all to do.

The author writes to members of God's household facing hard times and calls them to consider how to motivate others to show love and do good deeds. The Topical Lexicon states that this "speaks of weighing, discerning, or viewing with the intention of understanding and responding."[37] Considering how to spur others on can mean we take an interest in them (Phil. 2:3–4) and seek their good (1 Cor. 10:24). Trying to understand what they are going through (Rom. 12:15), we speak with kindness (Prov. 31:26). In other words, we genuinely get to know one another.

Whenever a new team member arrived, we devoted several hours to hearing their life story, starting with childhood and including all major events. We found out their strengths and weaknesses. We discovered their spiritual gifts. We learned if they were spontaneous or if they had to think about things first, if they liked to lead up front or help from the background, if they were outgoing or shy. We sought to know each other before making suggestions about ministry opportunities.

My teammate truly knew me. She understood that I needed lots of time to study and prepare for my events, that I'm detail-oriented, more gifted in discipleship than in evangelism, and more shy in a crowd. Because she paid attention to my personality, I realized she cared about me. So it was easier for me to accept her suggestions and ideas. She was "considering" me, not simply butting in or trying to control the way I served.

Our objective is to spur one another on to love and good deeds. This verb is also translated "provoke, motivate, stir up, or stimulate." When goading a horse to action, an actual spur can be uncomfortable. It sometimes irritates.

Author Lori Lipsky writes in her devotion in *Wit, Whimsy & Wisdom,* "[God] wants us to give careful thought and to plan how we might use our influence. He tells us to take conscious aim, focusing on specific ways we might prompt others to do good. We are to motivate those within our sphere of influence. We're to plan how we might stimulate them to be involved in acts of kindness."[38]

The apostle Paul spurred on his congregations by encouraging, comforting, and urging them to live lives worthy of God (1 Thess. 2:12). Our enthusiasm for a particular task can also be an effective "spur" (2 Cor. 9:2). My teammate was so excited about sharing the gospel and discipling others that I could not help but catch her vision and get on board. Her example excited me to act even though I often felt uncomfortable while doing so.

Looking back, I realize that I am who I am today largely because of my teammate. I tackled projects and took on ministries because she inspired me. I developed skills and confidence due to her belief in me. I have since tried to spur others on as she did with me. I intentionally attempt to understand them so well that I know what kind of good deeds to encourage them to try. I endeavor to serve the Lord so enthusiastically that others want to join me.

Read

Look up and meditate on the verses referenced above.
What is God saying to you about spurring others on?

Recount

Remember a time when God prompted you to spur someone on to love and good deeds. Who can you tell?

Respond

Merciful Lord, I confess that I don't often want to expend the energy necessary to consider how to spur on my brothers and sisters in the Lord. Give me eyes and ears to see them as you see them, to discern how to encourage them. Help me get so excited about my service to you that others will catch the joy and get on board. Show me who I can spur on today.

45

Pool Time

God Gives Us Laughter

> *Our mouths were filled with laughter, our tongues with songs of joy. Then it was said among the nations, "The LORD has done great things for them."*
> *Psalm 126:2*

Since we lived on an island replete with hotel resorts, we gathered almost every week beside a pool with teammates. To distinguish the pools at each location, our children named them—the "cave, bridge, slide, bubble, stage, sand, diving, wave, and mouth" pool. The kids loved the hours and hours they spent diving, jumping, climbing, and swimming with their friends.

One day we gathered at the "golf" pool, so named because it was (of course) adjacent to a golf course. As this was an all-day outing, we brought our own lunches and snacks. That day, our teammate had a whole bag of chocolate chips. These precious morsels were often hand-carried as a priority item in our carefully weighed luggage or as a requested gift from visitors.

At first, I was horrified that she would eat the chips straight out of the bag and not reserve them for cookies or other treats. Undeterred by my scorn, she spontaneously stood up, clutched her bag of chocolate chips to her heart, and invited us to her "chocolate-chip-oholics anonymous" support group.

I have tried many times to remember her exact words, but what she said really isn't the point. What mattered was that she made us laugh. Laughter so long and deep that tears flowed down our faces and our bellies ached. And that's exactly what we needed—a natural, life-giving relief from the stressful demands of our cross-cultural lives.

I wrote about all the fun, laughter, and play we enjoyed as a team in *Yet We Still Laugh:*

> How did we survive it all? We had times of fun, play, and laughter. They were short, but they were regular, and they were intense.
>
> We also visited various beaches or took hikes around local sites. We did touristy things. We showed up at bougie resorts insisting upon local prices to eat, enjoy the pool, and even stay overnight. We celebrated birthdays and holidays together. We played board games. We watched movies. We had fun.
>
> An afternoon by the pool, listening to our children imagine and play with each other while we sat and read or chatted and ate fun foods (like chocolate chips) proved paramount for helping us decompress from the struggles of the days before and prepare to tackle the challenges ahead. It broke barriers between us. We could not have survived the stress, let alone the crises, if not for the days we took away from the rings of the phone, the knocks on the door, and the cross-cultural demands of life.
>
> Even though we didn't have a manual to tell us how to do this, I am grateful to God that we innocently stumbled upon our practice of fun and laughter. Research has proven what we learned through experience—our mental and emotional well-being were improved, our blood pressure, stress, anger, and anxiety decreased. It strengthened our relationships, relieved our tensions, and thus enhanced our teamwork. I could even make the case that it improved our immune systems (we sure needed that) and added to our lifespan.
>
> God gave this gift to us through my husband, other teammates, our children, and our freedom to laugh at ourselves. I admit sometimes we gravitated into the realm of making fun of someone on the team or something in our host country, but we tried to keep the jokes only between us and apologize when necessary.
>
> Despite the challenges we experienced, I believe the psalmist sums up our team life: "Our mouths were filled with

laughter, our tongues with songs of joy. Then it was said among the nations, 'The LORD has done great things for them'" (Ps. 126:2).[39]

Read

Read Job 8:21; Proverbs 17:22; Ecclesiastes 3:4; Philippians 4:4. What do these verses tell you about joy and laughter?

Recount

Remember a time when God gave you laughter to endure hardship. Who might enjoy chuckling with you as you recount your fun experiences?

Respond

God my restorer, thank you for the gift of humor and laughter. Thank you for giving me a spouse, children, and team who helped me laugh and enjoy life. Please show me the humor in my current difficult situations, and teach me to laugh at myself when necessary.

46

My Happy Place

God Gives Us Gifts for Ministry

Therefore go and make disciples of all nations, baptizing them in the name of the Father and of the Son and of the Holy Spirit, and teaching them to obey everything I have commanded you. And surely I am with you always, to the very end of the age.
Matthew 28:19–20

The women of our national church planting team sat on the couch and chairs around me in our *tamu* (guest) receiving room. Tea and cookies adorned the coffee table. Open Bibles lay on our laps. This was my happy place. Here I could use my gifting and my passion to teach God's Word to these dear co-workers.

As we met weekly for Bible study, I became aware of their deep needs. I was often overwhelmed at the intensity of them. One lady declined any offers to minister outside the home. Another was neglecting to care for her family. Still another wanted to start a ministry that didn't enforce our team vision and required outside sponsorship.

I cried out to the Lord for wisdom to know how to help them. I invited them to turn to Ephesians 4:11–13:

> So Christ himself gave the apostles, the prophets, the evangelists, the pastors and teachers, to equip his people for works of service, so that the body of Christ may be built up until we all reach unity in the faith and in the knowledge of the Son of God and become mature, attaining to the whole measure of the fullness of Christ.

"This is my foundation for ministry," I shared. "God has given us gifts and abilities. Mine is teaching. And the purpose of my teaching is to equip you for service, and to build you up so that you become mature and live fully in Christ. I long for you to be mature. If you remain like an infant in your faith, you'll be tossed back and forth by everything you hear. I will speak the truth in love so that together we will become a unified body of Christ, building up each other in love, as we each do our work" (Eph 4:14–16).

In between our group Bible studies, I visited them in their homes. I wanted to grow closer to them. I desired a better understanding of their strengths and weaknesses and thus to ascertain how to encourage them.

On one visit, Sara expressed how my foundation for ministry had challenged her, especially the part about becoming spiritually mature instead of spoon-fed. In turn, I was encouraged to see her enthusiasm to minister to people, if only through bringing some dried fish to help supplement the meal of a poorer family. I encouraged her not to neglect her own husband and child while she served her community.

Over time, Nella's hunger for reading the Word increased. Olive was convicted about her tendency to rebel and not obey God's directives. After returning from an intense discipleship course, Mary tearfully recounted how she had learned she must forgive those against whom she harbored hatred.

Growth in these women was slow, but it manifested as I diligently discipled each one and they responded to the promptings of the Holy Spirit.

Read

Peruse Ephesians 4:11–16; Colossians 1:28–29.
What is God saying to you though these verses?

Recount

Bring to mind a time when God used you to disciple someone else, leading to their maturity. Who can you tell?

Respond

Creator God, thank you for the opportunities you bring to disciple others. I don't always feel adequate, and it can be overwhelming, but you will enable me to build others up, to help them reach maturity in their faith. Help them respond to your Spirit as he instructs and guides them.

47

Teammates

God Unifies His Body

Now you are the body of Christ,
and each one of you is a part of it.
1 Corinthians 12:27

I picked up the phone (again) to settle a misunderstanding with my teammate. She had shared her heart and frustration about a sensitive matter, and instead of simply letting her vent, I spoke up, challenging why she was so bothered. I blundered and used hurtful words, and it went from bad to worse. When she countered, I responded defensively. I needed to apologize.

Even though for the most part we had a wonderful, healthy team, we still faced relationship challenges. Still in my thirties, I was growing and maturing even as we served together. I was often careless with my words and body language and not aware of the hurtful messages I sometimes conveyed. I shed tears regularly as my team challenged and convicted me. Yet I needed them. After all, we were the body of Christ (Eph. 2:19).

We were brothers and sisters—a family joined by Jesus's blood—and he was our head (Col. 1:18). We had different kinds of gifts, but the same Holy Spirit was the source of them. While we served uniquely, we served one God. There were various ways to work, but the same God did the work through us (1 Cor. 12:4–6). We were individuals, but we were all necessary to the task and couldn't operate separately (1 Cor. 12:20–21). And most importantly, "there should be no division in the body" (1 Cor. 12:25) but rather equal concern for each other. If one part suffered (we had that part down), every part suffered with it. If one part was honored, every part rejoiced (1 Cor. 12:26).

Instead of concentrating on our challenges and differences, I determined to focus on how Jesus intended me to function as part of his body. He was my head whom I ultimately served—not my team. My part on the team was necessary but no more important than others' parts. If another member was honored, I was honored too. Because we were one body, I could not dismiss a sibling-in-Christ. We needed each of our contributions if we were to reach our goal of making God known (Isa. 26:8) on the island.

But I couldn't stop just at accepting my fellow teammates. Team life without love meant nothing (1 Cor. 12:31–13:3). In fact, loving my teammates was more important than all the combined contributions of our team. Loving them proved my love for God (1 John 4:21), and it demonstrated my faith to the community around me (John 13:35).

With this new understanding about living in the body of Christ, I asked the Holy Spirit to change me. I attempted to apologize even more quickly to my teammates and willingly see issues from their point of view. I didn't want to hurt my teammates, so I prayed to be more sensitive and think carefully before I spoke, to not offend, and to show love in tangible ways. I attempted to live what my husband once said, "We want to be team encouragers, not wreckers."

Read

Check out 1 Corinthians 12:1–13:3.
How can you show love above all else to your teammates?

Recount

Ponder a time when God unified your team. Who can you tell about this work of the Spirit?

Respond

Make us a unified team, Holy Spirit. While we may not have chosen our current teammates, they are our brothers and sisters in you. We are one body. Remind us that we need each other, that we cannot build your kingdom alone. And help us love each other because nothing shows love to a parent (you) more than seeing their children loving each other.

48

Internal Snags

God Works Despite Us

You are still worldly. For since there is jealousy and quarreling among you, are you not worldly? Are you not acting like mere humans?
1 Corinthians 3:3

It was one of those days when I wondered why in the world we had chosen to live on this island and if we would ever have any impact. Sometimes we felt more opposition from the local believers than we did from the majority religion.

Mark and his national friends had planned a songwriting workshop to be held in a local church. Three days before it was scheduled to take place, we hit a snag. The sponsoring arts group refused to allow the main songwriter to speak from the pulpit. Twenty years prior, he had been in prison (although falsely accused), and the sponsors feared that someone would catch wind of this and report them to local authorities.

In order to maintain unity, my husband sought a compromise. Perhaps the songwriter could share his information in some other creative fashion, via interview or panel discussion. But when the songwriter heard the opinion of the sponsors, he decided to withdraw. He was certain their fear proved their divergent vision.

Each side utilized Bible verses to back up their position. As a result, we were at a standstill. The workshop was cancelled. We were disappointed because these folks had tremendous potential, but they seemed more concerned about their own reputations than the name of God. The quarreling and pettiness of believers had stymied an evangelistic effort. The majority group didn't need to oppose our efforts as those within did enough damage.

My husband and I took our questions to the Lord. *Where are you in all of this conflict? Why have you not yet proclaimed your name here? Should we bypass this local congregation even though the church is supposed to be your means to reach the world?*

We wondered if God had perhaps protected us from some troublemakers who would have attended the workshop. Rather than inviting unknown attendees, maybe it was wiser to begin with folks who knew us and shared our burden for outreach. Maybe God had revealed the true motives of the arts group, exposing their divided hearts.

Whatever the reasons or the outcome, God reminded us of a few things through this experience. Before we judged others for their petty squabbles, we too had to put away our own agendas (Matt. 7:5). Due to the intensity of the spiritual battle we faced, we needed to be ready with our spiritual armor in place and strengthened by prayer (Eph. 6:11). Instead of allowing this setback to discourage us, we remembered the Lord chose to use us, imperfect as we are, and he would work out his plan despite us (2 Cor. 12:9).

Mark pivoted. He personally invited up to fifteen interested folks to join us in our home to learn the songs directly from the songwriter himself. Although a much smaller event than previously hoped for, in the end a few dedicated believers took away songs in their own language and style that they could use in evangelism and discipleship. Despite the initial setback, the Lord's name was indeed proclaimed.

Read

See Matthew 7:1–5; 2 Corinthians 10:3–5; 12:9–10; Ephesians 6:10–12.
What questions do you have for the Lord regarding your current ministry?
What is he saying to you?

Recount

Think of a time when God worked despite the internal quarrels of the church. To whom might you relay this reminder?

Respond

Compassionate Lord, thank you for choosing to use us imperfect humans. Thank you for building your kingdom despite the squabbles of the church. Teach me not to look with a judgmental eye on the faults of others but to see where I, too, am causing division. Build your kingdom, Lord, with or without us.

Week Nine

Liturgy During Personal Pain

Precious Father,
you already know what I'm going to say.
I've filled my journal with this for years.
I've shouted and cried, begged and bargained.
You know my pain, loss, fear, and disappointment.
Once again I ask, "Take it away please.
Give me what I desire and long for."

That one thing, that deeply private thing—
Why don't you make it better?
You seem to answer every prayer but this one.
You work mightily among the unreached
but not within the four walls of my home.

Personal issues feel the most painful, Lord.
Betrayal, broken trust, unmet needs, marriage struggles,
loved ones who don't follow you, choices our children make,
watching others suffer, letting go, choosing not to enable,
miscarriage and infertility, unwanted and invasive touch,
codependency, anxiety, depression, mental illness,
conflict, misunderstanding, name calling, threats.
The intimate stuff we can't share,
the hard questions we ask—or don't dare to.

Why me? It feels unfair. Why do I suffer and not another?
Why am I deprived and another rewarded?
I sacrificed to serve you and followed you to the ends of the earth,
I expected to suffer for the gospel, but not in this way.
I obeyed and took the narrow path,
so I want exemption from this kind of pain.

Yet Lord, I'm learning that you don't promise "yes" every time.
Sometimes your answer is slow,
a gradual path of growth and change,
other times we must wait for our perfected bodies
in the new earth.
I acknowledge that I don't see the whole picture,
I don't know how you're at work behind the scenes.

You promise that you are good, loving, kind, and compassionate.
You care, you hear, you comfort, you are involved,
you never leave me or abandon me,
you hear my cries and respond,
you feel my pain and mourn with me.

But I still live in a world that groans from the weight of sin,
I live with people who fight against their flesh as I battle my own.
I confess my self-centeredness, my doubt, my entitlement
while knowing that you graciously allow me
to speak the truth about my situation.

I lift up my soul to you—
all my anguish, complaints, anxiety, and sorrow.
Lord, bring help when I call, give me Scripture to cling to,
show me your presence, answer my questions, provide resources.

I admit that at first, all I wanted was for you to take away the pain
by filling my need immediately.
Gradually I came to see that my greatest need is to know you—
my source of life, joy, peace, love, and hope.
I hear your whisper above the pain,
"I love you, my child."

Amen.[40]

49

Broken Bones

God is With Us

By day the Lord directs his love, at night his song is with me
—a prayer to the God of my life.
Psalm 42:8

Everything's okay. It's not broken," my child's teacher said as she approached my car. "There is no bruising, and he can move his fingers."

I had just arrived to pick up my sons, only to see my eleven-year-old cradling his left arm. Lane had fallen off the monkey bars. Fortunately, he didn't have a lot of pain as long as he didn't move his arm a certain way.

Over the next few days, he still refused to shift his arm in that direction. Instead, he used his right arm to reposition his left arm. Questioning the teacher's diagnosis, my husband took him for an x-ray. Sure enough, his radius bone was broken about two inches above the wrist. It had snapped in two, and now one fragment sat on top of the other.

We immediately consulted our insurance company. The agent instructed us to fly to Singapore as soon as possible, especially since it had been three days since the break. We decided to go as a family and take advantage of an unexpected vacation.

It would be a long night, but the agent arranged everything. We arrived in Singapore around 8:00 p.m. and took a taxi directly to the doctor's office. He confirmed that Lane needed surgery. Even though it was now midnight, it could not wait until the morning. Everything moved quickly after that. We headed straight to the hospital where Lane was admitted and taken into surgery.

As the nurses prepped him, Lane looked at me anxiously, his eyes pleading for help. Our son had a heightened fear of needles and did not know what lay ahead. How does a mother respond to her child's plea? How do parents help their children face suffering and pain?

"Sing praise songs in your head," I told him.

Over the years, whenever our sons had trouble getting to sleep, woke during the night, or feared the dark, I instructed them to sing "in their head." Lane, in particular, was gifted musically and already knew many songs from his collection of children's music, school tunes, and the worship songs playing regularly in our home. This technique calmed him down and reminded him to think about God. It filled his mind with praise and worship.

Our brave boy did well overall. The doctor placed a titanium plate and five screws into his bone to reconnect the two broken pieces. Apart from some residual nausea from the anesthesia, all proceeded normally, and he was released the next afternoon. In between three follow-up visits, we ended up having quite a fun week.

The incident with my son's broken arm reminded me of my own broken bone on my first birthday in Papua New Guinea. Though I don't remember it, my parents tell the story of how I fell off our porch and consequently spent five weeks with my leg in traction in hospital. Having five other children 135 miles away to care for and following the medical advice of the early 1960s, my parents went home. While I know they loved me and must have been heartbroken to leave me, I weep for that little girl. Even though I believe they did what they thought best, as any parent has to at various times, I'm angry they made the decision they did. So I'm especially grateful I could be with Lane throughout his hospitalization.

When our children are all alone, and we can't do anything about it, or we are powerless to rescue them, or we don't even know they're in danger, our God is with them. When we must make decisions that benefit yet potentially distress our children, as my parents had to, God will come as a mighty warrior and be with them in the middle of their tragedy or trial.

God has since revealed to me in precious ways how he never left me during my recovery. And like I now know that God was present with me even before I realized it, Lane knows that God was and is with him as he continues to sing songs "in this head" to this day.

Read

Look up Deuteronomy 31:6; 2 Chronicles 20:20–22; Psalm 135:1–3; Zephaniah 3:17.
What do these verses tell you about singing and God's presence when anxiety hits?

Recount

Remember a time when God helped you overcome your fear through the gift of music. Who can you tell about this experience?

Respond

Omnipresent One, thank you for being with my son in his anxious moments. Thank you for providing medical care, even if we had to travel to receive it. Thank you for music and praise to help him overcome fear. Teach me to turn to you in praise when facing my own anxiety.

50

Unwanted Touch

God Values Us

Those who look to him are radiant;
their faces are never covered with shame.
Psalm 34:5

As I recovered from the stressful cesarean section of my second delivery (see entry 62), I missed the comfortable, pillow-filled, automated bed I had enjoyed during my first delivery in the U.S. I yearned for the walk-in shower and my mother's bedside assistance. This time around I had to gingerly scoot off the bed and hobble over to a plastic chair for a nurse's aide to give me a wipe-down bath.

She chatted freely while she wiped my arms. "*Apakah air susu Ibu sudah keluar* (Has your breast milk come in yet)?"

Wait. What? Possessing only basic language skills at the time, I failed to immediately comprehend what she had just said. In the seconds that it took for me to register her words and formulate my response, her hand shot out, grabbed my breast, and squeezed.

"*Belum* (Not yet)," she said blithely as she continued washing my forearm, oblivious of what she had done.

I sat in shock. What had just happened? Did she really just do that? As my sore breast throbbed, I had no words. Caught off guard, I had not suspected such action.

This woman, while doing her innocuous job, had invaded my privacy. She had touched a part of me that is reserved for a very particular few. Perhaps she felt she qualified as a "medical professional" to measure my milk supply. But more likely she was simply curious and unaware she had breached my personal space.

I was grateful that this unwanted touch was a small matter and not lastingly harmful. Yet it represented a huge cultural divide and a larger reality of life on the field—for I know that others have not gotten off so lightly and instead, suffered immensely from unsolicited touch.

Sadly, the intrusion into the private spaces of global workers and their children by house helpers, teachers, and friends happens all too frequently. I've heard stories of neighborhood children and schoolmates pulling down the pants of boys to check if they are circumcised. Children touch each other's private parts while playing. Adult caretakers fondle genitals in an attempt to soothe babies. Young girls are pinched and grabbed. Hands roam up skirts to grope women and down shirts to fondle breasts on public transportation or in the marketplace. Men too are propositioned and touched inappropriately. Even though we take every precaution possible in our demeanor, dress, and attitude, global messengers still experience such invasive assaults.

I wish I could go back and respond differently. I might have swung my freshly bathed arm and swatted the nurse's aide in the face! In a more Christ-like manner, I would attempt to explain that her behavior was unacceptable for me, personally. I would acknowledge her action as a form of assault. I would process it with others. I would do more to cultivate a team culture where we could discuss unwanted touch and intrusive acts together.

Most importantly, I would emphasize that God does not want his children to be treated this way. He sees us. He understands our shock and pain. We are his beautiful children created in his image. He mourns with us while reminding us of our invaluable worth. We can believe what God says about us rather than taking on shame because of the actions of others.[41]

Read

Read Genesis 1:26–27; 16:13; Deuteronomy 7:7; Psalm 34:5; 139:13–14; Isaiah 43:4.
What do these verses tell you about how God values you?

Recount

Think back to a time when God's esteemed value of you helped you overcome the effects of unwanted touch. Who would be safe enough to tell?

Respond

Lord my healer, you say that I am your beloved daughter, precious and valued in your sight. No matter what others may say about me or how they may violate me, show me your grace and goodness. Heal any part of me tainted by the way others view me or have treated me.

51

Unmet Needs

God Will Complete His Work

And I am certain that God, who began the good work within you, will continue his work until it is finally finished on the day when Christ Jesus returns.
Philippians 1:6 (NLT)

We experienced various trials during our years overseas. But by far the most difficult was a deeply personal one, not revealed to others. As a new bride, I had become aware that my husband could not love me in the ways I had expected. Gradually I learned that, due to childhood trauma, he dealt with acute anxiety. He developed unhealthy coping behaviors which in turn affected me.

I knew Mark loved me, and I could identify many positive and healthy aspects to our relationship. Yet because he couldn't love me in the ways I hoped for, I felt alone and rejected. I begged God to heal him, to take his struggles away. I filled journals with my hurts. I cried often. I tried to fix it myself by being everything he needed. I manipulated and schemed for his attention.

Ten years into our marriage, Mark reached a crisis. His anxiety had increased to the point of panic attacks and depression. Our gracious team relieved him of his duties for a time, and we returned to the U.S. to receive help. He turned a corner those weeks as the Spirit flooded Mark with his love and presence. At the same time God touched a place of deep hurt in my heart, tenderly saying, "Let me give you what I know you need, not what you think you want."

I had wanted God to take away all our problems instantly. But instead, he answered with slow healing, in both of us, over many years. A few trusted folks knew the depth of our pain and supported us in our healing journey, but mostly God continued to lead us step-by-step through books, a visiting counselor, an understanding friend who offered hope, a conference, a prayer partner, even a dream.

Over time, God taught me to apply many helpful truths mostly through the daily disciplines of prayer and Bible study. Primarily, I took my husband off the throne of my heart (see entry 24). I let go of control over my marriage and instead let God satisfy my needs and fill my heart with himself. I released my disappointment and hurt to God over and over and allowed him to fill me with love for my spouse. My patience grew as I waited for God to work in Mark in his time, in his way. I learned to serve Mark purely out of love, not just so that he'd serve me in return.

A key lesson was identifying the lies the enemy told me and replacing them with truth. When I thought I'd never get to enjoy the relationship I desired, God told me he'd graciously give me all things (1 Tim. 6:17). When I complained that Mark wasn't trying hard enough, God told me that love believes all things (1 Cor. 13:7). When I felt that my own struggle had no purpose, he replied that he would produce fruit in me (Gal. 6:9). When I felt unloved, God tenderly told me I was his treasure (Ps. 45:11). When I felt I could no longer wait for resolution, he reminded me love is patient (1 Cor. 13:4). And when I was convinced that my spouse would never change, God told me he would complete the good work that he had begun in Mark (Phil. 1:6).

If I had known how long this healing journey would take, I would have given up. But God in his mercy revealed only one step at a time—the insight, the spiritual truth, or the adjustment that I needed each moment. My deep pain became the foremost means by which God produced compassion, grace, kindness, and empathy in me.

As God continued his work in me, he did the same for Mark. Mark came through his refining process more in the image of his savior as evidenced by his own words:

> Suffering involves the inner turmoil of the process of becoming Christlike. In this regard, the daily choice of dying to my own desires and choosing Christ enacts God's will in my life through the path of suffering.

Our healing journey continues. There is still more to learn. Not all my desires will likely ever be fulfilled this side of heaven. But I have reached a place of contentment in Christ.

Read

Look up and meditate on the verses above.
What is God saying to you about the deeply personal issue you cannot speak about publicly?

Recount

Write about when God kept working in you through the deepest pain. Who might be encouraged by your story?

Respond

Holy Lord, I trust you and put my hope in your transforming power. I allow you to work in my spouse in your way and your time frame. I realize and accept that life with pain is normal, but that it is not wasted. Use the pain to complete your good work in me and my spouse. You did not promise a trouble-free life, but you did promise you would never leave me and would be sufficient for all that I need.

52

Miscarriage

God Does Not Punish Us

> *"Neither this man nor his parents sinned," said Jesus, "but this happened so that the works of God might be displayed in him."*
> *John 9:3*

"I suggest you prepare yourself for losing this baby," the gynecologist warned gently. "I can't find a heartbeat."

Alarmed, I tried to comprehend this sudden turn of events. I hadn't even had my first appointment, and now here I lay on an examining table—on my thirty-first birthday, in Indonesia, at 9:00 p.m.—beginning to miscarry.

Accepting the reality of this pregnancy had been difficult. I had delayed taking a test and telling others because the timing didn't fit my plans. But God had determined I should have a third child, so I relinquished control and accepted his gift. Now this surrender added to my confusion. *How could this be happening now? Did I do something wrong?*

I continued to bleed throughout the night and started cramping in the early morning hours. I knew in my heart this was the end. I silently spoke to my unborn child:

Goodbye, little one. I am sorry that I didn't want to be pregnant at first, that my body is rejecting you. Now, when I am about to lose you, I am incredibly sad. I regret that I will never know you, hold you to my breast, watch your first smile, or hear you coo. But I will always love you. Goodbye, dear one.

I also talked to God: *Is there something wrong with me or the baby? Did my body repel it because my heart wasn't enthusiastic? Why would you give only to take away so soon? Are you punishing me for not wanting another child right now?*

By morning, contractions had begun and my doctor proceeded with a dilation and curettage to clear my uterine lining. The procedure done, he emerged from the operating room, shoved a kidney-shaped stainless-steel dish under my husband's nose and asked, "Do you want to bury it?" In the container lay a two-inch fetus—too small to see the gender but formed enough to know it was a tiny human. Shaken, he declined.

This presentation of the fetus reminded me that I was giving birth in a foreign country, and that fact led to even more questions. We had not discussed how to react in a case like this. *What did they do with my baby? Should we have taken it home with us since we were unaware of the local protocol for disposal? Had I been a careless mother?*

Since I had no answers to these queries, I proceeded as usual and plowed ahead. I devoted little time to processing my loss. I rationalized that losing this baby was not a big deal because it was unplanned and I wasn't emotionally attached to it yet. In addition, I already had two sons that I deeply loved, and we still had time for another child. I simply accepted this miscarriage as God's will for me.

However, as each month, then each year, passed without any signs of another child, the loss of our number three swept over me with renewed force. Finally during a routine annual physical, a nurse wrote "infertile" on my chart after hearing my history. In one stark word, it was final.

Like before, more questions emerged—this time tinged with guilt. *Was I unable to conceive because I had not wanted to be pregnant? Had something happened during the uterine procedure? Did I fail to ask the right questions or trust too much in the doctor? Would this have happened if I had been in my home country?*

Over the years, the wondering and the mourning haven't ended, but they are now framed in time and experience that taught me to trust God. I can look forward to the day when I will fully know my third child and we will spend eternity together.

I have also learned that grief comes in stages, as the processing of my miscarriage touched my life in different ways over time. First, the night when I said goodbye to my unknown child. Then the years I desired another child and could not get pregnant. Later, while enjoying adult children and wishing there were more around the table. To this day I mourn every time I recount this story.

And so, to my thirty-one-year-old self, I declare: "Take time to grieve. This is a legitimate loss even if you don't realize it. You can mourn and be grateful at the same time. Your feelings of guilt, inconvenience, and frustration are normal. Go ahead and ask your questions because God knows what he's doing. He is not punishing you but loves you deeply. Trust his plan, wisdom, and goodness. He has reasons you cannot imagine when he chooses to bring a little one into his arms. He declares every life miraculous no matter how long they live.[42]

Read

Skim John 9:1–41.
What do these verses reveal about God and his interaction with us in times of loss?

Recount

Recount a time when you learned that God was not punishing you when you lost someone or something dear to you.

Respond

Thank you, sovereign Lord, for teaching me how to grieve, even if long after the fact. I release my doubts and guilt to you, trusting that someday you will reveal to me the reasons behind this loss. I receive your love, knowing you did not take my baby to punish me.

53

Lack of Fit

God Has Good Work Prepared for Us

> *For we are God's handiwork, created in Christ Jesus to do good works, which God prepared in advance for us to do.*
> *Ephesians 2:10*

Every year at our regional conference, we held a video competition. These fun parodies of each other and our strange life were the highlight of the week. I can proudly say that my husband and I, together with our friends, won first prize several times.

Our first team leader and his wife, however, usually brought the most laughs. Each year, they picked a couple and played them chit-chatting in their bed, wearing pajamas. One year, my husband and I were the subject of choice. She made fun of my propensity to can cucumbers by crunching on pickles directly out of a jar. He strummed a few bars on a *kecapi* (an instrument like a zither), copying Mark's role on the team as champion of traditional music.

"But I don't even like the local music" he declared.

Perhaps we found it funny because it was true. Mark really didn't enjoy this music nor this particular role. At least once a year, I listened to Mark's misgivings. *I don't think I can do this. Why am I even here? I don't like the local music, which is why the government has granted me a visa. I'm not passionate about church planting like the other guys. I'm a terrible global messenger.*

In short, Mark struggled to find his niche as a church planter. While we had supportive teammates with a common goal, we each focused on a singular aspect of our strategy. Without a daily companion, he floundered. Many days he simply "gritted his teeth" and did what was expected of him. Ever in search of a more perfect fit, he devised strategies for different visas, batted around ideas, brainstormed outlets for ministry, and explored outside-the-box ventures.

I didn't know how to respond to his questions. All his ideas. His seemingly insatiable need for change. I wanted stability and consistency. I worried and stressed and asked my own questions. *Did Mark's regular changes in role mean he was wishy-washy? A quitter? Even worse, was he being unfaithful to his calling? What does faithfulness mean anyway?*

About ten years into the journey, our team completed a gifting and strengths assessment during an annual retreat. When the coach tabulated Mark's profile, she said, "According to your assessment, church planting might be rather difficult for you. Your gift mix indicates people-helping fields, such as counseling."

Her declaration brought instant understanding. Mark got along well with all kinds of people. He was approachable and thus often became the go-between on our team. People came to him for encouragement and advice. He understood the patterns of pain and suffering. He had even studied psychology as an undergrad student. Now Mark realized his strengths lay on the other side of church planting, in an actual church where he could lead worship, disciple, and counsel members of the body.

As Mark had his epiphany, so did I. Needing change and preferring consistency were personality traits—two different ways to approach life, neither good nor bad. Mark's nature craved variety and starting new things. He thrived on developing something from scratch or improving an existing system. He needed a partner to help carry out his ideas—or someone to give them over to.

As I came to better understand my husband's personality, I learned not to stress out every time he suggested a change or expressed his questions for the umpteenth time. He needed space to process and vent. I needed to listen more and talk less. He desired creative outlets for his ideas, but I could offer realistic help to carry them out.

Looking back, I believe Mark exhibited what the author of Hebrews describes:

> We want each of you to show this same diligence to the very end, so that what you hope for may be fully realized. We do not want you to become lazy, but to imitate those who through faith and patience inherit what has been promised. (Heb. 6:11–12)

Switching roles, changing strategies, even eventually leaving the field did not mean my husband was unfaithful to his team, his employer, or to the Lord, because faithfulness is about following Jesus, not about our vocation. It's about being diligent to the end and exhibiting great faith. Mark did that. Through all the ups and downs of finding his fit, he remained steadfast in his allegiance to God and his overall mission.

Read

Peruse Matthew 28:18–20; Romans 12:6–8; Colossians 3:11–17; Hebrews 6:10–20.
What do these verses tell you about your niche?

Recount

Recall a time when God revealed to you the good work he had prepared for you to do. How might you incorporate this story into your mentoring of others?

Respond

Sufficient Father, thank you for creating a unique good work for each of us to bring to your kingdom-building venture. Help me to continue understanding my spouse's and teammates' bents so that I can encourage and build them up. Show me how to be faithful to you until my last breath.

54

Burnout

God Refreshes Us

Then [Elijah] lay down under the bush and fell asleep. All at once an angel touched him and said, "Get up and eat." He looked around, and there by his head was some bread baked over hot coals, and a jar of water. He ate and drank and then lay down again. The angel of the LORD came back a second time and touched him and said, "Get up and eat, for the journey is too much for you."
1 Kings 19:5–7

Entries such as this one made frequent appearances in my journals and letters to family:

> We are already living at such a high level of stress on a daily basis that we don't know what normal life is anymore. Mark has constant GI problems, partly anxiety- and stress-related. I worry that the boys will absorb his stress and not have a normal childhood. Is this the enemy's last-ditch struggle before the harvest? Can I believe there will be a harvest? What is God doing? Is it time for all of us to step away? Can we endure another tragedy?

We were a mess. But God was not. He graciously ministered to us and sent help exactly when we needed it. Once, help came in the form of a counselor from the U.S. who met with us and patiently listened to our story and our hearts. He confirmed that Mark and I had a wonderfully supportive team. Then he diagnosed our complete exhaustion and prescribed rest. He said, "If you do not pull back from some responsibilities and take time to heal, you are in danger of burnout."

He opened his Bible and read to us the story of Elijah (1 Kings 18–19). Even though the prophet had demonstrated that Jehovah was superior to the false god of Baal, his victory was cut short. Even though God had answered his (not the queen's prophets') prayer for rain after serious drought, he could not rest. Elijah had humiliated and destroyed Queen Jezebel's prophets, and she was livid. Nothing short of killing Elijah herself would satisfy her wrath. Now physically exhausted from the showdown with the false prophets and running faster than chariots, Elijah could no longer withstand Jezebel's threat. Quaking with fear, he hid in the wilderness and prayed to die.

> He came to a broom bush, sat down under it and prayed that he might die. "I have had enough, LORD," he said. "Take my life; I am no better than my ancestors." (1 Kings 19:4)

Our kind counselor reminded us that God did not rebuke Elijah for his despair but rather let him enjoy a deep sleep. When Elijah woke, God provided food and drink. But Elijah was still weary, so he slept again, woke, and ate a second time. God tended to his physical needs first before sending him on another long journey. Then Elijah heard the voice of God (1 Kings 19:9).

"God cares about your physical needs," the counselor said. "Take time to rest. It's permissible and necessary." As Mark and I listened to his life-giving advice, we both wept.

Acting on his recommendation, we took a Christmas trip to Singapore. We visited parks, went to movies, ate good food, frequented coffee shops, and enjoyed freedom from ministry demands. Mark also received some needed medical attention. Taking this time to rest made space not only for our bodies to be refreshed, but also for the Lord to renew our spirits and speak to us through his Word.

God ministered to me through the practice of rejoicing and finding strength in him. I experienced "the oil of joy instead of mourning, and a garment of praise instead of a spirit of despair" (Isa. 61:3). God turned my mourning into gladness and gave comfort and joy instead of sorrow (Jer. 31:13). As I faced returning to the island, the joy of the Lord was my strength (Neh. 8:10). I deliberately chose to rejoice in hope, persevere in tribulation, and be faithful in prayer (Rom. 12:12). But I only latched onto these truths because I took the time to rest and recuperate.

Read

Skim through Isaiah 18–19.
What is God saying to you about your need for rest?

Recount

Recollect a time when God ministered to you through a time of much-needed or even forced rest. With whom can you share your example?

Respond

Kind Father, thank you for giving priority to my physical body and need for food, drink, and sleep. Show me how to create regular rhythms of restorative rest for my body. Help me to stay consistent in caring for my body's needs so that I can continue to serve you and have the space and capacity to hear your voice.

Week Ten

Liturgy for Mourning a Loved One

Precious Lord Jesus, my dear friend and co-laborer has died.
I now understand what your disciples
must have felt when you were in the tomb—

Shock and disbelief. Did this really happen?
How? How could the Messiah die?
Anger. At the injustice, the cruelty, at themselves
for not stopping it, at God for letting it happen.
Disappointment. That Jesus didn't fulfill their plans,
build his kingdom, or display his mighty power.

Guilt. For running away and hiding,
for not being there, for not doing enough to save him.
Grief and sadness. At watching him suffer,
at losing a friend, a dream, at the (apparent) victory of the enemy.
Helplessness. Because they couldn't stop the pain,
save him from death, or usher in the kingdom.

Fear. That they would be next to die. So they hid.
Afraid to be bold, speak up, come out of hiding, or even stay put.
Shame. That they had followed a vain hope,
that they should've known better.
Moral Injury. Because they watched and
could not stop the cruel, unjust death of an innocent man.

Like the disciples, I wonder why my friend was taken so soon?
I feel the same emotions and feelings.
I weep in grief, disbelief, and anger.

I confess, Lord, that grieving has made me irritable.
I can only think of my own pain
rather than consider the needs of others.
I admit I'm assuming others are criticizing me.
I just want to be alone,
I have little energy
to take care of my own family.

Help me release my hurt and anger
and pay attention to others who also grieve.
Even in my numbness, help me serve them.
Give me grace to accept their varied reactions as they too grieve.

Thank you, Lord, for those who ministered to me as I mourned,
for the one who asked what life-giving activity
would soothe my soul, then created space so I could do it.
And for the others who prayed for me,
affirming my relationship with the one I lost,
validating my role in her life.
Their words brought healing to my soul.

Lord, like the disciples, all I can do is make preparations
to lay her body to rest, honor her, remember her, and wait.

And while the disciples did not realize
your resurrection was coming,
I know it has, and I can remember your words,
Your promises that you will come again,
that my friend will also live again,
that she is released from suffering and evil,
at peace and at rest.

Thank you for showing me what the disciples soon learned—
there is more to the story. It isn't over. You are indeed risen.

Amen.[43]

55

Preschool

God Opens New Paths

The Lord is my shepherd, I lack nothing. He makes me lie down in green pastures, he leads me beside quiet waters, he refreshes my soul. He guides me along the right paths for his name's sake.
Psalm 23:1–3

My close local friend, Nella,[44] dreamed of running a children's home or orphanage. To that end, she received training in establishing and operating village preschools as an avenue for gospel presence and proclamation. She had a real gift with children, especially those more disadvantaged. They flocked to her fun and winsome personality. Her smile and quick wit put them at ease. And the fact that they could almost look at her eye-to-eye only added to her appeal.

Nella spent her first year on the island learning local culture, making friends, and surveying local villages for a possible preschool location. Her first request to open a preschool was denied. All the restrictions of the educational system, the government, and the overreach of Islam frustrated her. However, she did not allow these obstacles to stop her from pursuing her goal—to share her faith by offering early education to those who could not afford to send their children to a regular preschool program.

Finally, she located the perfect spot in a remote Muslim village. She traveled one hour each way through a winding mountain pass three or four times a week to lay the foundation for her preschool. She discussed the concept with village heads, won over interested parents, and registered potential students.

At first, everyone welcomed her, even though they knew she was a Christian. Most understood her sincere desire to help their children and improve their standard of living. Heartened, she filed the required paperwork with government officials and raised the necessary funds.

Soon opposition arose. "We know your plan. You want to 'Christianize' our whole village. We'll be watching you."

Nella knew she served a big God and, with his help, could actually "Christianize" the whole province. Undaunted, she and I prayed for the government's approval of her proposal to reside in the village and begin teaching.

But God didn't answer our prayers the way we thought he should. Once again, her request was denied. Nella cried for days. I cried with her. I didn't totally understand her situation nor her personal needs, but God did. While I felt inadequate, I knew that in my weakness my heavenly Father would be strong. I couldn't tell her what to do, but I could listen to the Lord and relay his encouragement.

As Nella and I prayed and read God's Word together, the Spirit brought Joseph, Moses, and Rahab to mind. In each case, God's path wasn't the obvious or immediate one. After a lifetime of injustice and trial, God made something good out of Joseph's suffering (Gen. 50:20). God waited years and years for the right man—Moses—to deliver the Israelites from slavery (Exod. 12:41). And he went to great lengths to save Rahab from the destruction of an entire city (Josh. 6:25).

These examples reassured Nella that her good God would redeem this setback. Even though the rejection of her proposal meant she would have to pivot, it did not negate her mission. While she waited in faith for God to open a new way to start her school, Nella followed up with relationships, visited children, and looked for opportunities to share the good news in her neighborhood. She hosted parties and showed *The Jesus Film*. She continued serving children in new and creative ways.

Read

Read Proverbs 3:5–6; Isaiah 43:16,19; Habakkuk 1:5.
What do these verses tell you about God?
What is he saying to you?

Recount

Recall a time when God opened an alternate path for you to fulfill your mission after a door was closed. Who can you tell?

Respond

My deliverer, I loved the time I had with Nella each week, praying, reading the Bible, and watching her grow. I saw you answer prayers, helping me know what to say to encourage her. Remind me that as you guided all those years ago, you will again show me how to fulfill my current mission. When my plans are thwarted, open a new path for me to proclaim your truth.

56

Take My Life

God Gives Boldness to Speak

Pray also for me, that whenever I speak, words may be given me so that I will fearlessly make known the mystery of the gospel.
Ephesians 6:19

After Nella's two requests to start her own preschool in a Muslim village were denied, she tried a different tactic. Why not join an existing school? After months of prayer, she landed a job in an Islamic private preschool in a village which boasted of the purity of its religion.

In addition to reading and writing, Nella taught hygiene and health to her sixty four- and-five-year-olds. Each week she cooked a nutritious meal for them. She also provided clothing and toothbrushes for these underprivileged children. Mostly, she modeled the love of Christ.

But when the governing board realized their vibrant new teacher was a Christian, they wanted her gone. Lacking a valid excuse to fire her, they resorted to the local *shaman's* black magic.

A few days later, Nella told me, "I had a horrible dream last night. A ghostlike figure with the head of a bird and the body of a boy tried to strangle me. I began to sing, 'Jesus, you're the good shepherd,' and it left me. When I woke up the next morning, I found the head of a bird on the floor outside my bedroom. At first, I didn't think about it, but on the way to work, I realized the bird on the floor was the same as the bird in my dream."

When Nella arrived at the preschool, everyone registered

shock and surprise to see her. A co-worker quickly hugged her. "Thank goodness you are alive," she said with relief.

"What do you mean?" Nella asked. "Why are you worried?"

"The school officials paid a *shaman* to curse and kill you through black magic," she explained. "In fact, they've already tried four times!"

When the curses failed, the Muslim leaders sent Nella to a government official for questioning. Before her interrogation, I prayed Jesus's promise over her:

> But when they arrest you, do not worry about what to say or how to say it. At that time you will be given what to say, for it will not be you speaking, but the Spirit of your Father speaking through you. (Matt. 10:19–20)

God answered our request for boldness, and the Holy Spirit gave Nella confident responses to satisfy the official's probing questions. Still the school leaders remained desperate to get rid of Nella. They asked the *shaman* to curse her again, but this time, the medicine man refused, saying, "She's too strong. She has a power I cannot touch."[45] Her accusers were silenced. In the end, Nella was just told not to return.

This third rejection only increased Nella's resolution and boldness to tell children about Jesus. She would not back down. She was ready to face anything. "If more curses are put on me, if a riot happens again, if I never get to open a preschool," she said, "I'm staying put. Let them take my things. Let them even take my life. I'll just go to be with Jesus."

Read

Look up Luke 12:11–12; Luke 21:12–19; Ephesians 6:19. How do these verses encourage you to speak up boldly?

Recount

When has God given you boldness in the face of opposition or words to say when you were interrogated? Who can you share this with?

Respond

Precious Lord, thank you for Nella's example of bold faith. Thank you for her heart that simply wanted to help children and show them Jesus's love. Thank you for her perseverance through obstacles and setbacks. Help me to trust you like she did. I want to be able to say, "Take my life, for I would gain Christ" (Phil. 1:21).

57

Persevere in Suffering

God Does Not Waste Our Pain

> *Not only so, but we also rejoice in our sufferings,*
> *because we know that suffering produces perseverance;*
> *perseverance, character; and character, hope.*
> *Romans 5:3–4*

Nella seemed to suffer frequently. She complained of constant battles with health, first with severe menstrual discomfort. Then, for several months she had unexplained fevers. She required emergency surgery for appendicitis. Another time she was sick with a gum infection and subsequently had low blood pressure after eating poorly for almost a month. Even more seriously, Nella suffered a concussion, causing severe headaches, and was housebound for about six weeks.

In addition to her physical maladies, Nella dealt with loneliness since she had no partner in life or in ministry. She experienced separation from family, lack of material goods, frequent hindrances to her ministry, loss of friends, and little fruit from her labors. Once her home was robbed during the night, but she and her valuables were locked in her room, and she slept through the whole event. Despite it all, Nella wanted more than anything to please God and follow his will.

Feeling helpless yet wanting to encourage her, I suggested we look at the life of the apostle Paul as described in the book of Acts. We dove in, reading and discussing a few verses during our weekly mentoring meetings.

On Paul's first missionary journey, he was opposed by a

sorcerer (Acts 13:8), expelled from town (13:50), plotted against (14:5), and stoned and dragged out of the city (14:19).

On his second missionary journey, Paul was flogged and thrown into prison (16:23). He escaped rioting mobs (17:5), was opposed by his own people (18:6), and attacked (18:12–13).

On his third missionary journey, he was seized, arrested, and threatened with death (21:27; 23:12). Paul faced prison (24:27), trial (25:6–7), shipwreck (27:27), snakebite (28:3–4), and house arrest (28:16).

In his letters, Paul describes his daily life: weak, dishonored, hungry and thirsty, in rags, brutally treated, homeless, cursed, persecuted, slandered, harassed at every turn, facing conflicts on the outside, fears within (2 Cor. 7:5–6)—basically he was considered the scum of the earth (1 Cor. 4:11–13).

As we studied all these trials, Nella not only saw that suffering characterized all ministry, but she also learned that she did not suffer in vain:

> [God] comforts us in our troubles, so that we can comfort those in any trouble with the comfort we ourselves receive from God. (2 Cor. 1:4)
>
> And because of my chains, most of the brothers and sisters have become confident in the Lord and dare all the more to proclaim the gospel without fear. (Phil. 1:14)
>
> All this is evidence that God's judgment is right, and as a result you will be counted worthy of the kingdom of God, for which you are suffering. (2 Thess. 1:5)
>
> I want to know Christ—yes, to know the power of his resurrection and participation in his sufferings, becoming like him in his death. (Phil. 3:10)

God's Word sank into Nella's heart. She said to me, "You know, we too quickly blame the enemy for the trials that happen in our lives." I agreed. What about God's discipline and pruning, the evil of mankind, unsanitary conditions, or our own stubbornness or dumb mistakes? Both Nella and I became convinced that if the apostle Paul could endure his suffering for a higher purpose, then we, too, could rejoice that God was shaping our character through our hardships.

Read

Review 2 Corinthians 11.
What is God saying about the purpose for your current suffering?

Recount

Who might be encouraged to hear about a time when you suffered greatly and God revealed the purpose of your pain?

Respond

Spirit, my Comforter, thank you for the example of Paul who felt honored to suffer for you. Teach me to know you better through my suffering. Show me your comfort so that I might be more equipped to comfort others in their troubles.

58

Grace, Not Works

God Saves Through Faith

> *For it is by grace you have been saved, through faith*
> *—and this is not from yourselves, it is the gift of God*
> *—not by works, so that no one can boast.*
> *Ephesians 2:8–9*

Nella came to me distraught. She had just read Jesus's words in the Gospel of Matthew and was certain she did not measure up.

> "Not everyone who says to me, 'Lord, Lord,' will enter the kingdom of heaven, but only the one who does the will of my Father who is in heaven. Many will say to me on that day, 'Lord, Lord, did we not prophesy in your name and in your name drive out demons and in your name perform many miracles?' Then I will tell them plainly, 'I never knew you. Away from me, you evildoers!'" (Matt. 7:21–23)

She shared her struggles with me. Worried that she had failed to obey God somehow—such as not reading her Bible each morning or giving to a needy beggar at her gate—she feared God would say, "I do not know you" (Matt. 7:23).

I was confused. How could Nella fear she hadn't served the Lord enough? And did she really believe her acts of service determined her salvation? Even though she could no longer teach in an actual preschool, Nella still served needy children. She hosted a tutoring club in her home two afternoons a week. About ten children attended to receive help with homework, drawing lessons, reading practice, or just to play with her toys and read her books and magazines. She told stories about Jesus. She also facilitated a sponsorship program helping fourteen children receive food, soap, toothbrushes, and monthly school fees.[46] She even befriended a fifteen-year-old orphan girl and led her to Christ. Nella obviously loved Jesus and served him.

Concerned, I prayed with Nella and pointed her to pertinent scriptures to remind her of God's grace, that her acceptance into God's kingdom did not depend on her good deeds. I gave her various verses to study:

> He has saved us and called us to a holy life—not because of anything we have done but because of his own purpose and grace. (2 Tim. 1:9)

> For sin shall no longer be your master, because you are not under the law, but under grace. (Rom. 6:14)

> Therefore, there is now no condemnation for those who are in Christ Jesus. (Rom. 8:1)

> Let us draw near to God with a sincere heart and with the full assurance that faith brings, having our hearts sprinkled to cleanse us from a guilty conscience and having our bodies washed with pure water. (Heb. 10:22)

The day after Nella's thirty-fourth birthday, we met for our regular ladies' Bible study. Afterwards, I spontaneously asked her to stay for lunch and help me with a task. We chatted about her ministry and her family. I brought up the subject of her struggle with self-condemnation and doubt. She explained that God's Word had ministered to her and that she was at peace.

This would be my last visit with Nella.

Read

Look up and meditate on the verses above.
What is God saying to you to calm any doubts you may have about your deeds or lack thereof?

Recount

Record a story about when God reminded you that you cannot earn your salvation by the things you do. Who might need to hear they can stop striving?

Respond

Gracious Savior, when doubts and accusations flood my mind, remind me that it's not up to me to do enough good to gain your approval. Show me where I still attempt to save myself rather than accept your grace by faith.

59

Open Hands

God Shepherds Us Through Death

The righteous are taken away to be spared from evil.
Those who walk uprightly enter into peace;
they find rest as they lie in death.
Isaiah 57:1–2

We returned from a day at the beach on March 20, 2002. Our helper immediately met us at the car and handed the phone receiver to my husband. Our teammate relayed the dreadful news that Nella had collapsed that morning from severe head pain and now lay unconscious in the hospital.

I jumped back into the car and headed off to be with her. Once alone, I banged my fist on the steering wheel and expressed my worry and frustration out loud to the Lord: "Again, Lord? Now what? How many more lives will it take, Lord, to build your church on this island? Is this battle going to go on until one side retreats? Well, the enemy can just give up because we aren't going to!"

"It's really bad," my teammate said as I approached Nella's hospital room. "When she collapsed this morning, she also vomited and fluid filled her lungs. She has been fighting for breath all day."

I entered the room to see my sweet friend lying on the bed, blood and fluid coming out of her mouth, eyes glazed over. I sensed the tender voice of God deep in my soul, "Up to this point, you have held her with open hands. Now it is time to let her go."

"Take her or spare her as you wish," I replied. I knew that the valiant efforts of the nursing staff would do little to preserve her life. After she took her last breath, peace flooded her face. I stood by her bed along with many others who loved her dearly, and I prayed, "Lord, you could raise her up again. You are capable, and I believe you can."

The gentle voice of my Father responded, "Eva, would you really ask her to leave my presence and come back to that world of suffering? I have released Nella from her pain, her loneliness, her struggle, her self-doubt, and instead, I have brought her into my arms and given her complete joy and happiness. Is that not kindness?"

"I know she is far better off with you, Lord," I said in my heart.

I viewed death as something so final. In Nella's case, a waste of a young life lived fervently for God. But God sees death as a continuation of fellowship with him. God stood beside Nella holding her hand, calling her name, and joyfully accompanying her to her heavenly home. He didn't leave her or forsake her but desired her presence with him. Not early, not late—at just the right time.

Nella's favorite Scripture was Psalm 23. She now dwells in the house of her Lord forever (Ps. 23:6). She entered into his joy (Matt. 25:23). She heard him say, "Well done" (Matt. 25:21). She no longer suffers physical pain or strives to establish a preschool. She no longer worries if she is doing enough good for the kingdom. She has finished her race and kept the faith (2 Tim. 4:7). She has entered into rest and found peace (Isa. 57:2).

Read

Open up your Bible to Psalm 23.
How might this psalm comfort you through your valley of death?

Recount

When did your good shepherd lead someone you love through the valley of death? How might you memorialize their life?

Respond

Good Shepherd, teach me to hold my dearest loved ones with an open hand and to desire your will for their lives, not mine. Help me to realize that your kindness may mean deliverance to death. My heart grieves as I miss their smiles, their touch, their presence, but at the same time I thank you for the many ways they faithfully served you and enriched my life.

60

Rejoicing Faith

God Enables Us to Reject

Do not grieve, for the joy of the Lord is your strength.
Nehemiah 8:10

I missed Nella's friendship, smile, humor, enthusiasm, and fun. Stressed out after her death, I struggled with knowing how to move forward or process the multiple losses of the past few years. I don't remember what brought it to mind, but I dusted off a small devotional on my bookshelf, something I had received while studying at Columbia International University and taken overseas. *Are You Rejoicing?*, a 31-day devotional written by Joy Ridderhof, greatly aided my healing process.

Joy Ridderhof was one of CIU's most famous alumni. She recounted, "In 1936 I returned home from Honduras ill in body, disqualified for future missionary service and without financial support. It was a dark picture indeed. Then God's Word spoke to my heart, 'Rejoice, Joy, rejoice.' Rejoice? Why? God is working all these things together for your good. He has a wonderful purpose for your life.'"[47]

Following this, Ridderhof founded Gospel Recordings with the goal of recording the message of salvation in every language in the world. But she was equally known for practicing "rejoicing faith" while deep in adversity. She exhorted, "Make it your choice to rejoice." These words from her devotional encouraged me:

> When we rejoice in tribulation, we receive far greater benefits than otherwise could be possible. Our Lord is made glad as well, and others seeing us are also encouraged to rejoice.[48]

> Rejoice, and make every one of these trials a springboard for blessing and fruitfulness. Even when it's not in you to do it, by His Spirit, count it all joy.[49]
>
> Bitterness cannot take root where joy and a spirit of thankfulness are rampant.[50]
>
> When you are asking for a victory which only God can bring, then rest—and let faith sing.[51]
>
> Let the song of praise arise from hearts that trust when all outward circumstances make us want to groan.[52]
>
> We can praise God in trials and sorrow and suffering and bewilderment because we understand the nature of God—that He delights to work in ways far above our human understanding.[53]
>
> Worry is the enemy's weapon to defeat us, but worry cannot hold out against joy![54]

Following Joy's example, I chose to find things to rejoice about and give thanks for. First, and most importantly, our names (mine, Nella's, Anna's) were written in heaven (Luke 10:20), and God loved each us deeply and lavishly (Ps. 31:7). I rejoiced in God's promises (Ps. 119:162), specifically that I would see my dear friends again one day. I also rejoiced that my faith was being refined through the fire of grief (1 Pet. 1:6). And I was extremely glad that neither of these lovely women had to suffer pain anymore.

Another item of good news worth celebrating was new life (Isa. 65:18). The day before Nella died, her teammate gave birth to a baby girl. As I looked around me, I rejoiced in the miracle (Luke 19:37) that a new believer was soon to be baptized. I also had a supportive and wonderful team and five other local women to love and love me back.

I especially resonated with the prophet Habakkuk's call to rejoice in the middle of his calamity. Like him, I told my soul, "I *will* rejoice!" I found it helpful to rewrite Habakkuk 3:17–19 in my own words:

> Even though my friend Nella is gone, even though I can no longer hear her laughter and see her smile, even though she

> can no longer minister to the children who flock around her, even though we have lost a vital member of our team, I will rejoice in the Lord. I will be joyful in God my Savior. The sovereign Lord is my strength. He leads me to the place of joy and victory.

The discipline of rejoicing was neither a quick fix nor a denial of the grief I felt but rather a tool to process my sadness. Choosing to rejoice did not mean I reveled in the grief or was glad my friend had died. Rather my joy was "in and of the Lord," and as such, it realigned my focus and perspective. As I read Joy Ridderhof's devotional and studied Bible verses pertaining to rejoicing, giving thanks, and worshipping, the grief and despair slowly lifted.

Read

See Psalm 94:17–19; Proverbs 17:22; Romans 5:3; Philippians 4:4. Rewrite Habakkuk 3:17–19 in your own words.

Recount

Recall a time when God helped you rejoice while facing adversity or grief. Who might be helped by hearing your story?

Respond

Lord, my overcomer, thank you for showing me the power of rejoicing while grieving. Show me what I can rejoice about every day. Make me into a grateful person who chooses to be glad and exercises rejoicing faith in you and your promises.

Week Eleven

Liturgy for Family Life Overseas

Lord God, building a family doesn't happen automatically.
Maintaining marital unity takes work, and
growing little humans requires constant attention.
For now, it's my primary task no matter where I live in the world.

But doing this while navigating a foreign environment
doubles the challenge.
It takes so much time and energy just to survive;
to plan menus, find food sources, sanitize
lettuce and cucumbers, light the stove, wash the dishes—
all to fill the mouths depending on me for everything.

And that's just meals, Lord.
Procuring diapers, wipes, bottles, and bibs exhausts me,
fighting the dirt and germs feels futile,
finding medical care is confusing.
And then there's clothing, education,
socialization, comfort, love, security.

Keeping the kids alive consumes me,
leaving little time for the one I want to invest in most.
My spouse is also figuring out life,
trying to help me parent well and fulfill the expectations
of our team, leadership, church, local government.
I'm worried I'm neglecting him.

Father God, I feel anxious about failing my family,
or the work, or both.
I'm worried that I'm ruining them
or adding irreversible strain to my marriage.
I believed it would be easier once we had landed and settled in,
but instead I feel overwhelmed and incompetent.
Tasks that felt second nature now feel alien.

So Lord, I confess my fears and anxieties.
I remember that you promise to give wisdom if I ask.
I ask, Lord, today and every moment,
for discernment, understanding, and the ability to
train and disciple my children,
love and support my husband,
as well as find my own avenues to serve
outside these four walls.

I remind myself that you, Jesus, are the true head of our home.
I first get my nourishment, love, security, and hope in you,
not in my husband's abilities or my children's behavior.
Lead me to sink my roots deep into you so I will grow in love,
fill me with yourself so I don't depend on my family to fill me,
but instead serve them humbly and selflessly.

For my family, I pray—
Fill us with the knowledge of your will
in all wisdom and spiritual understanding,
teach us to put on compassion, kindness,
humility, gentleness, and patience,
help us forbear annoyances in one another and forgive offenses.
Above all else, increase our love and unity,
and let your peace rule in our home.

Amen. [55]

61

Vacation Blues

God Cares for Us

Cast all your anxiety on him because he cares for you.
1 Peter 5:7

After making it through unit one of language study with relatively few hiccups, we made plans for a restful staycation to get more settled and familiar with our city and community. A trip to the zoo with some new friends in the neighborhood seemed the perfect way to start the week.

To say I was unprepared for this experience is an understatement. In retrospect I realize I had never been to a zoo outside of the U.S. Even during my childhood in Papua New Guinea, the one animal sanctuary I had visited was lush and green and well kept. I was completely caught off guard for the culture shock that bombarded me that day.

Trash and filth lay everywhere. A dull roar deafened our ears. People crowded around us, and beggars with outstretched hands blocked our path. The combined smells of warm bodies, animal feces, and rotting food assaulted our senses.

And then there were the animals. The poor creatures lay in dirty, inhumane conditions looking dejected. Instead of feeling joy and warm fuzzies at watching cute animals, I felt horror viewing them in their cramped cages. Where I had expected the animals to energize me, their plight drained me.

Soon the stares of other visitors, the finger pointing, and the giggles directed at our son in his backpack on this father's back took center stage. Looking around, I noticed there was not another such carrier in sight. We had inadvertently set up our son and ourselves to be more on display than the animals.

In addition to the stress and anxiety produced by the zoo and the crowd, I worried about our son. Our usually active and happy boy was lethargic, whiny, and burning up with heat. All things considered, I just wanted to get away from that stinky, horrible, exposed place and protect my child. Sensitive to our dilemma, our friends arranged for an early return home. Sure enough, our baby had a fever, severe diarrhea, and a remainder of his previous chest infection.

For the rest of our vacation, I continued changing runny diapers, treating a bright red bottom, and tending my ailing child. I was frustrated with ineffective medication and language barriers which hindered my ability to find the help I required.

I felt utterly helpless and vulnerable. *My little guy didn't ask to be brought to this place. What if I ruined him for life? Both physically and emotionally? What if he never got better?* When my son wasn't well or when I could not control his health, I dissolved into an anxious, tense, unhappy mess. It felt like the enemy was coming at me through my ill son.

When I reached my lowest point, a verse we memorized in our recent Indonesian language class came to mind and helped calm my anxiety. I repeated it over and over again.

> *Jangan kwatir tentang hidupku.* (Don't worry about your life. Luke 12:22)

I also remembered an exhortation I'd recently heard from a visiting speaker. Our team leader's mother, Carol Richardson[56], told us, "When we dwell on fears and let them grow into dreadful imaginations, we must take those thoughts captive and hand them over to the Lord" (2 Cor. 10:5).

In considering God's promise to care for me and my son, I found I could trust him. In taking my fearful thoughts captive, I could relax. Thankfully, after another round of medication, our baby improved. I was so relieved and grateful for God's care.

Read

Read Luke 12:22–23; 2 Corinthians 10:5; 1 Peter 5:7.
What do these verses say about God's care for you and your children?

Recount

Think of when God cared for you through your worst week ever. Who can you tell about God's precious provision?

Respond

Faithful Lord, thank you for caring for me and my family. Help me to trust that you will provide all we need. Help me to take my thoughts captive, to not let my imagination about what could be morph into debilitating anxiety.

62

C-Section Lamaze

God Grants Us Offspring

Children are a gift of the LORD; they are a reward from him.
Psalm 127:3 (NLT)

Three months after arriving in the country, we learned we were expecting our second child. I was a bit apprehensive because during my first pregnancy I developed pre-eclampsia[57] (high blood pressure and protein in the urine) in the 37th week. Seven days of bed rest followed, then ten hours of induction, and finally a cesarean section. Thankfully, I delivered a healthy, albeit borderline-low-birthweight, son.

Now I faced giving birth in a new country, this time with minimal language skills. Several other women on our team had already delivered babies in our city, so they pointed me to a doctor they trusted.

All seemed well until my 28th week checkup revealed a very low and irregular fetal heart rate. I sent an urgent request to our network of prayer partners and tried to rein in my thoughts from extreme scenarios. To my relief, at the next wellness visit, our baby's heart beat normally again. But six weeks later things ramped up again.

Our child was in breech position. The doctor turned him once, but our baby promptly returned. He tried two other times unsuccessfully (and uncomfortably). The doctor was willing to attempt a vaginal birth if the baby wasn't too large. So we waited and prayed again.

A week before my due date, pre-eclampsia reared again. The

doctor prescribed bed rest, medication, and self-monitoring my blood pressure. But seven days later, with my blood pressure still elevated, the baby still breech, and its weight above the cutoff, a cesarean section was the best practice.

The next day I lay on an operating table in an outdated, yet clean and air-conditioned, birthing clinic. The anesthesiologist allowed only one extra person in the room, so Mark and I opted for our teammate, a nurse, to accompany me. Mark stood outside the door and watched through the window.

After administering the medicine, the anesthesiologist pricked the right side of my abdomen. "I can feel that," I told him. The epidural, which had been a success during my first cesarean, didn't work so well this time. My left side was sufficiently numb but not my right side. So he increased the dose and we waited. Finally, after about half an hour, he administered an additional local anesthesia and began the surgery.

At that point everything was a blur. I remember hearing a baby cry and someone saying, "It's a boy." I remember someone asking me if I wanted to see him and noticing a fat red face.

But mostly I remember the pain. "What's going on?" I gasped in my grogginess.

"The doctor is stitching you up, but your anesthetic is wearing off. Breathe with me," my nurse teammate stated calmly. The pain increased, and we began more intense Lamaze-style breathing. After about five minutes, the quick-thinking anesthesiologist knocked me fully out.

"Where am I?" I queried when I came to fifteen minutes later.

As the drug wore off, my teammate explained, "You're the only woman I know who's had to do Lamaze breathing during a c-section."

While initially disappointed that I had not "given birth naturally," I soon became grateful for my healthy sons. And for modern medicine. I thought of underprivileged women who did not have access to this life-saving procedure nor could afford it.

While my experience of giving birth overseas presented some unique challenges, the outcome was a healthy baby. However, this is not always the case. A colleague left the country because their newborn needed serious medical attention not available on site. Another expat in town lost a baby due to full eclampsia. Some of my teammates were unable to have children. A few never even had the opportunity to choose to have them.

Every child is a gift, a miracle, no matter the location or circumstances. But thankfully biological children are not the only offspring God gives us. Adoption, fostering, and being an "aunt and uncle" to our friends' children also brings great blessing. And then there's the spiritual children God grants us as we disciple other believers and help raise mentees to maturity in Christ.

Read

Look up Psalm 139:13–16; Proverbs 17:6; John 16:20–21; Galatians 4:19–20; 1 Timothy 1:2
What is God's view of children?
What spiritual children have you birthed?

Recount

Bring to mind a time when God helped you birth someone (or something) special. Why don't you tell that person their "birth" story?

Respond

Faithful Provider of good gifts, thank you for the safe delivery of my two sons even though we were at risk. Please comfort mothers whose childbirth experiences have not ended in joy. Provide needed medical care to women everywhere. And for those who have no biological children, please multiply their spiritual children.

63

The Best Mommy

God Gives Wisdom to Parent Well

If any of you lacks wisdom, you should ask God,
who gives generously to all without finding fault,
and it will be given to you.
James 1:5

The sign read, "Where's the best mommy?" My two sons, ages three and five, happily followed their dad on a Mother's Day hunt to find the best mommy.

My husband took them to the local KFC, where they ran around looking in cupboards and under seats while my husband videoed them with a mammoth VCR recorder popular in the '90s.

"Is that the best Mommy?" Dad asked as he pointed to a statue of Colonel Sanders.

"No!" the boys screamed, "That's a daddy."

"Is she the best Mommy?" Dad discreetly pointed to a woman working behind the counter.

"No!" The boys ignored her and moved on in their search.

Next Dad took them to a grocery store, and the boys ran up and down the aisles, looking behind stacks of pots. "She's not here," they announced.

My eldest son looked in a trash can. "She's not in the garbage."

Lastly, Dad took them outside to a guard post where the boys climbed up on the benches. They looked down at the ditch flowing with nasty run-off water, trash, and filth.

In his toddler voice that still could not say his "r's," my

youngest announced, "She's not in the poopy wadder."

Unsuccessful in their search, Dad finally took them back home. When they arrived, they entered the kitchen where Mom (me) was savoring the silence while preparing dinner.

"Is that the best Mommy?" Dad asked.

"Yes!" They ran to me, and we embraced.

Later they showed me the video of their adventure. What a treasure it was. We still love watching it to this day. And what an honor to be a mom to such precious boys.

I endeavored to live worthy of their young love and be the mother that each of them needed. To do that I required the wisdom of the Lord, the ultimate parent. And I learned the practice of asking for his wisdom from my own mother. Like when I held my firstborn in my arms fresh from the hospital and dissolved into tears of frustration. "Mom, I don't know how to raise a child."

"None of us know," my mother replied. "But the Bible says, 'If any of you lacks wisdom, you should ask God, who gives generously to all without finding fault, and it will be given to you'" (James 1:5).

This principle of asking for wisdom turned out to be especially beneficial when we added living in a foreign context into the mix of parenting. God never failed to give me ideas, resources, advice, and help when I asked for it. When I felt incompetent, he was my competence (2 Cor. 3:5) to mother my children well.

Read

Peruse Isaiah 41:20; 54:13; 66:13; 2 Corinthians 3:5; Galatians 5:22–23.

How do these verses relate to parenting?

For what parenting situation do you need wisdom?

Recount

Reminisce about a time when God gave you wisdom to "parent" a child in your care. How could you tell them about it?

Respond

Perfect Father, I remember with fondness the days when my sons thought I was the best. They are grown now, but I still endeavor to be the best mother they need for every stage of their life. Continue to give me wisdom to parent my adult children well.

64

For Hugging

Jesus Touches Us

For this is what the Lord Almighty says: ". . .
Whoever touches you touches the apple of his eye."
Zechariah 2:8

One morning while I was studying my Bible lesson in my bedroom, my four-your-old son ran in and flopped down on the bed next to me. Uncharacteristically, he did not speak.

"How are you, buddy?" I asked.

"Fine," he replied with a smile.

"Do you need anything?" I asked.

"Yes," he answered.

"What do you need?" I expected that he wanted me to make a snack or help build a train track.

"I need you for hugging," he said.

"I need you for hugging too," I said as we embraced. "Mommies need hugs too."

Having been reassured, he got down from the bed and ran off to play.

A hug. That's all my son needed. It was a way for him to feel safe and loved. A way for me to demonstrate how our heavenly Father "gathers the lambs in his arms and carries them close to his heart" (Isa. 40:11).

We all need hugs. We need human touch. Author Stephen W. Smith says, "Through touch, we communicate love, affection, devotion, appreciation, value, and acceptance. The soul longs to touch and be touched, embrace and be embraced."[58]

I thought of Jesus who broke all cultural and religious rules and often touched the diseased, the blind, the deaf, the terrified. Jesus brought comfort and healing through touch.

> Jesus reached out his hand and touched the man. "I am willing," he said. "Be clean!" Immediately he was cleansed of his leprosy. (Matt. 8:3)
>
> Jesus had compassion on them and touched their eyes. Immediately they received their sight and followed him. (Matt. 20:34)
>
> Jesus put his fingers into the man's ears. Then he spit and touched the man's tongue. He looked up to heaven and with a deep sigh said to him, "Ephphatha!" (which means "Be opened!"). At this, the man's ears were opened, his tongue was loosened and he began to speak plainly. (Mark 7:33–35)
>
> While he was still speaking, a bright cloud covered them, and a voice from the cloud said, "This is my Son, whom I love; with him I am well pleased. Listen to him!" When the disciples heard this, they fell facedown to the ground, terrified. But Jesus came and touched them. "Get up," he said. "Don't be afraid." (Matt. 17:5–7)
>
> People were also bringing babies to Jesus for him to place his hands on them. (Luke 18:15)
>
> After that, he poured water into a basin and began to wash his disciples' feet, drying them with the towel that was wrapped around him. (John 13:5)

As my son went on his way, I wondered who else might need my touch? For instance, when our team gathered to pray, I could place my hands on the shoulders or touch the arm of the one I prayed for (Acts 13:3). I could embrace those who were single on my team since they often went days without any human touch. I asked the Lord to help me remember that the next time I extended my hand, I was touching someone with the same touch of the God who deeply loves them.

Read

Check out Isaiah 40:11; Luke 15:17–21; Acts 20:36–38. Meditate on the verses above.
What do these verses tell you about God?
How might you give a sacred touch to another today?

Recount

Recount a time when God touched you through the hands of another. Resolve to tell them how much that meant to you.

Respond

Lord Jesus, thank you for your touch that I feel through the hands of my fellow believers. Give me wisdom to know when and how to extend a sacred touch to a fellow traveler. Help me to point them to you, the true healer and comforter.

65

Mommy Lit a Candle

Jesus is Our Light

You are the light of the world. A town built on a hill cannot be hidden. Neither do people light a lamp and put it under a bowl. Instead they put it on its stand, and it gives light to everyone in the house. In the same way, let your light shine before others, that they may see your good deeds and glorify your Father in heaven.
Matthew 5:14–16

I woke with a start. The electricity was off again! The stillness felt suffocating and the darkness overwhelming. All was silent. No whirring from the fans. No moving air directed upon our faces. No cool air from the primary luxury we allowed ourselves. Not even the dim beam of the streetlights outside.

Several times a month our electricity went off during the night (and during the day for that matter). When it did, the darkness was absolute unless it was a full moon or starry night. Without a fan or air conditioning, the humid air smothered us.

I didn't want my two boys to wake up in the dark and feel alone and frightened. So I rose from my bed and lit some candles throughout the house. If they woke up or needed to use the bathroom, they would have light to guide their way.

My husband thought this ritual a bit extreme, worthy of some levity. Mark is musical and composes little ditties and fun songs. One day, while playing around on his keyboard, he composed the words, "*My Mommy lit a can-dle, so I wouldn't be afraid.*" The song stuck and became a family joke, a symbol of overprotectiveness but also of loving care.

These nights also became symbolic of the spiritually dark climate surrounding us. In Scripture, light overcomes darkness (John 1:5), conquers fear (Ps. 27:1), exposes hidden motives (1 Cor. 4:5), and produces the fruit of goodness, righteousness, and truth (Eph. 5:9). Jesus tells us he is the ultimate light.

> When Jesus spoke again to the people, he said, "I am the light of the world. Whoever follows me will never walk in darkness, but will have the light of life." (John 8:12)

> In him was life, and that life was the light of all mankind. The light shines in the darkness, and the darkness has not overcome it. (John 1:4–5)

Jesus leads us out of darkness (John 12:46), displays God's glory (2 Cor. 4:6), brings light and truth to those living in darkness (John 3:19–21), and reveals the way to salvation (Luke 2:30–32). As he is the light, we who follow him now shine his light (Matt. 5:14–16).

We attempted to be the light of Jesus to our neighborhood. In particular, I tried to radiate good deeds, goodness, righteousness, and truth to my house helper (see entry 68). I'm not sure how brightly we shone, but we were mindful of reflecting the Light of the world every day.

Read

Meditate on the verses above.
What is God saying to you?
What can you learn about God and light from these verses?

Recount

Describe a time when God enabled you to shine his light to someone else.
Who might be encouraged by your testimony?

Respond

Light of the World, sometimes I don't feel like my light is burning very brightly. But you remind me that light shines brightest in very dark places. Help me to live in such a way that my neighbors will see your light and glorify you.

66

Parenting Doubts

God Can Be Trusted with Our Children

Trust in the Lord *with all your heart and lean not on your own understanding; in all your ways submit to him, and he will make your paths straight.*
Proverbs 3:5–6

Some days I felt I had totally failed at parenting. I was inconsistent in enforcing family standards and correcting negative behavior. I didn't lead devotions with the boys every day. I was lax to push them to work longer or give them more difficult tasks. I lost patience with them and didn't maintain control of my reactions at the end of the day when everyone was tired. (Of course, parenting was a joint effort with my husband, but since these were my doubts, I won't speak for him.)

I fretted about whether they would ever be independent enough to entertain themselves or make their own choices. *Would they imitate the more aggressive local social norms, or follow the Muslim god, or bow to peer pressure? Was I modeling enough, praying enough, praising enough, giving enough attention? How would I know if I had successfully raised them?* I prayed and prayed, filling my journals with these questions and fears, trying to trust God and not lean on my own understanding.

I was most uncertain in the realm of educating our sons. I disliked homeschooling yet didn't want to release control of the process. I worried that they would not graduate from high school let alone college. I tended to do some of the work for them instead of motivating them to complete it themselves. If nothing else, I did successfully teach them both to read, one of their favorite pastimes to this day.

When a "national-plus" school—a hybrid of Indonesian and English education, local and expat teachers—opened on our island, we wondered about enrolling them. (The boys were in first and third grades at the time.) We knew this wasn't a perfect solution and that it would come with challenges. And it also was pricey, but my in-laws agreed to help fund the tuition.

For weeks, the school decision consumed my thoughts. I struggled with letting them go for so many hours a day. I wanted to shield them from challenging situations and possible hurt. *What if the experience scarred them for life?* To have my children impacted by circumstances beyond my control is one thing. Being the cause of their pain because of my own decisions is another matter entirely.

My husband and I prayed, discussed, and consulted others. In the end, we knew enrolling them in the new school was the best decision. I decided to give my fears and worries to the Lord. After all, the struggle about best options for educating our kids would be the same no matter where we lived. Bottomline, did I trust my heavenly Father, that he would take care of my boys?

I wrote out verse after verse of prayers for my precious sons. As I dropped them off at school each day, I pictured God's angels on either side of them. As they walked into their classroom, I whispered: *Keep them from false teaching, from physical harm, and from emotional abuse.* On the drive home, I kept praying. And throughout the day. Every school day.

One day I panicked when my son asked, "How do we know we are following the right religion?" Another time I was sad when his brother expressed fear of praying publicly in Jesus's name. I was proud when they questioned whether they should participate in singing a Muslim song of worship. These experiences provided key teaching moments, giving them freedom to question, express their fears, and experience God's help themselves.

Over time, I realized that when I overly shielded my sons from hard situations, they missed out on opportunities to rely on their heavenly Father. In my guarded world they might succeed with their natural abilities, but not necessarily by any faith of their own.

My dependence on God grew as I sought his wisdom to

guide, protect, and advise them. I confessed my tendency to look at circumstantial evidence as the basis for parenting success—perfect behavior, a peaceful day, an observed schedule—rather than the character of my children's hearts or the evidence of the fruit of the Spirit in their lives.

My sons told me years later that these days were difficult for them. Perhaps it wasn't the best situation, but we bathed their school environment in prayer. A few years later we repatriated to the U.S. where my discipline of praying continued. And now we can testify that by God's grace and mercy, our wonderful adult sons honor, love, and follow him.

Read

Look up Psalm 37:5; Isaiah 26:3; 49:25; 54:13; Philippians 4:6–7; Hebrews 11:1.
In what ways might you need to trust God with your children?

Recount

Record a story of when God proved trustworthy with your children. Who can you tell about it?

Respond

Keep my children safe, oh God. Teach them to take refuge in you. Show them that apart from you, they have no good thing. Help them see that troubles multiply for those who chase after other gods. Counsel them, instruct them, keep their eyes on you so they won't be shaken. Make known to them the path of life, and fill them with joy in your presence (Ps. 16).

Week Twelve

Liturgy for Guidance

Holy Spirit, what is this restlessness?
What are you saying?
In what direction are you nudging?
Is it time for a final goodbye?
What would that even look like?
How do we know this is your leading?

I look to you, for you are my guide.
You lead me in the way I should go.
But the way ahead looks cloudy, the process messy.
Whatever I decide, someone will be affected.

I reaffirm my belief that you are good,
and your will is pleasing and perfect.
I utter the "Prayer of Indifference"—
I am indifferent to anything but your will—
not seeking your stamp of approval on my plans
but resolving to obey you when I know your plans.

I want to remain or leave in accordance with your will.
In order to test and know what that is,
I first offer myself as a living sacrifice and
let you transform me.
I renew my mind by focusing on your truth.

Increase my ability to hear your voice.
You speak in multiple ways,
help me listen to all of them.

Speak me to me through your Word,
give me specific verses and
confirm them in numerous ways.

Lead through circumstances,
through "open and closed doors,"
provide opportunities to serve,
show me what's next.

Counsel through the confirmation of others.
As I talk to pastors and mentors, reveal the way to go,
use even strangers to steer me
and impress their words on my spirit, Lord.

Speak in your still small voice,
teach me to listen to the whispers of God,
stamp on my heart and mind what you want for me,
teach me to draw close to you and quiet my heart.

Lord, you created me with talents, passions, and desires
so that they might be used to serve others.
Direct me to where my desires match yours.

Guide by your peace that this is the way to go.
Peace doesn't guarantee ease, but it means
my heart will be confident to go forward.

Show the way even through your creation,
speak through nature, visions, dreams,
confirm over and over that it is your voice I hear.

I choose to listen to the voice that syncs with Scripture,
I choose the way that causes me to exalt Jesus,
love him more, trust him more, love others more.

"Lord, show me your ways, teach me your paths.
Guide me into your truth and teach me.
For you are the God who delivers me;
I rely on you all day long." (Ps. 25:4–5)

"Speak, for your servant is listening." (1 Sam. 3:10)

Amen.[59]

67

Rock Removal

God Makes the Seed Grow

I planted the seed, Apollos watered it,
but God has been making it grow.
1 Corinthians 3:6

"Our work in Indonesia," my husband explained to a friend and prayer partner, "is simply to plant seeds. Like the farmer in Jesus's parable of the sower (Luke 8:5–11), we scatter the seed of the Word of God. Jesus said that seeds planted in rocky soil will wither and that those planted in thorny soil will be choked out. But the seeds planted in good soil will produce a crop a hundred times more than was sown."

Before Mark could go any farther, our listener interrupted with an incredulous look, "Planting seeds? I thought you guys were still removing rocks."

"Rock removal?" Mark replied. "Of course! That describes our ministry perfectly. The soil isn't nearly ready to receive seeds."

My husband grew up in fertile farming country. He knew that effective farmers took time to prepare the soil before sowing seeds. They cleared the land, overturned clods of dirt, removed rocks, plowed up the ground, and mixed in fertilizer. These necessary steps ensured seeds embedded in rich, good soil. Proper preparation yielded a greater harvest.

We began to contemplate what "rock removal" looked like in our context. Primarily it meant praying for God's Spirit to move over the island, to open eyes blinded by the enemy (Acts 26:18), to soften hearts hardened by sin (Heb. 3:8), and to unplug ears deaf to the truth (Isa. 35:4–6). We prayed that the islanders would "come to their senses" and recognize Satan's deceit (2 Tim. 2:26), that God would remove the blindness from their minds (2 Cor. 4:4) and open a door for our message (Col. 4:3).

Living Christ-like lives was another way to remove rocks (1 John 2:6). We could show our host community that we were not like the foul-mouthed and immoral foreigners depicted on movie and TV screens. Treating our helpers fairly and kindly and working diligently for our local employer also displayed our Christian character.

Removing obstacles to the gospel also meant demonstrating the love of Christ (John 13:35) by giving rice to beggars, supporting children who could not go to school, and providing heart medication for a friend who could not afford it (1 Pet. 2:12).

My husband and I never saw a harvest during our time of service overseas, but we plowed ahead, knowing in faith it would come someday. We knew at the time that we removed rocks exactly where God had placed us, and so we were content to be obedient to his call.

As we continued to move heavy "rocks," I was encouraged by the words of the prophet Jeremiah:

> Blessed is the one who trusts in the LORD, whose confidence is in him. He will be like a tree planted by the water that sends out its roots by the stream. It does not fear when heat comes; its leaves are always green. It has no worries in a year of drought and never fails to bear fruit. (Jer. 17:7–8)

We had God's assurance that what we sowed would bear fruit. We believed that he would make the seed grow (1 Cor. 3:7) as we prepared the soil for the seeds of the gospel.

Read

Look up and meditate on the verses above.
What does "removing rocks" and "preparing soil" look like in your context?

Recount

Recount a time when God helped you prepare the soil for the seed of the gospel even when you saw no results. Who might need to hear this encouragement from you today?

Respond

Lord of Hosts, serving you can get wearisome. I so want to see a harvest, to witness results from my labor. Removing rocks or killing thorns doesn't seem very glamorous. Planting individual seeds is so tedious. I'd love to see the harvest, to reap the fruits of my labor. Help me to be patient and faithful in the task you have given me today.

68

Sharing With Sue

The Spirit Leads Us to Share the Gospel

How, then, can they call on the one they have not believed in?
And how can they believe in the one of whom
they have not heard? And how can they hear
without someone preaching to them?
Romans 10:14

Most of the time, I did not feel like an effective global messenger on a church planting team. I wasn't a natural evangelist. I spent most of my time at home with two active boys, trying to maintain order and guide their education. The only local non-believer I interacted with regularly was Sue, our helper. She watched me daily in my home as I attempted to live congruently with my faith, to demonstrate a place where love reigned overall.

The first time Sue and I talked about our different systems of belief, she commented, "Your religion is simpler than mine."

"Yes," I replied, "it may look simpler because following Jesus is a relationship of faith, not a set of rules to follow. I could actually never *do* enough to earn salvation. That's why Jesus made a way for me to be saved."

"This is the first time I have ever heard that we cannot earn salvation," Sue responded.

I did not expect Sue to believe in Jesus right then. Since she considered that community, culture, and fate determined her religion—not logic—it did not even enter her mind that she might make a faith choice for herself.

Over time, opportunities arose to talk about forgiveness, mutual respect, and sacrificial love. I emphasized that since Jesus taught these concepts, we could only live them out with his help.

One night I dreamed Sue died, and as I comforted her husband and wept, I was overcome with the realization that I had not yet clearly told her the plan of salvation. When I woke, I felt God urging me to share the good news as soon as possible.

A few days later Sue and I chatted while she washed dishes. "Thank you for teaching me so much," she said.

I replied, "I'm grateful I have been able to show you many things, but I have not yet told you what I believe is the most important thing," I said. "God's holy book says that you need to hear this in order to believe (Rom. 10:14)." I then proceeded to explain God's free gift of salvation offered to us through Christ's death and resurrection.

Soon after that Sue agreed to listen as I read chronological stories from the Sunday school curriculum I was writing for Muslim background believer's children. While she cut up vegetables or washed dishes, she listened, corrected my grammar, and pointed out confusing content.

Then the Bible translation project needed another checker. Sue consented to read the Gospels of Luke and John in her heart language and translate them back into Indonesian for checking purposes. After 9/11, I sensed an urgency to tell Sue about my source of hope, that no matter what happened in the future, she could know God and be saved.

"I would love to read the Bible and pray with you," I offered. In response, Sue cried.

We met as often as possible to read. She eagerly learned anything I taught and even began reading the Bible on her own. She became more open to the gospel than ever before. I prayed that the Holy Spirit would cause her to ask for further explanations. A month later, she asked me, "What do I do with all that I'm hearing?"

Next Sue watched both *The Jesus Film* and the story of the prodigal son on TV. Finally, I asked her if she was ready to believe.

"What do you think about everything you are learning?" I asked Sue.

"I don't know what to do with Jesus," she replied.

"If you will seek the truth, God will show it to you," I answered.

I realized then that it would likely take years and many more explanations for Sue to choose to follow Jesus. To date, I do not know if she has believed in him. I take comfort in knowing that I obediently planted the seed. Others have watered that seed since I left. I continue to pray and trust that God will produce his harvest in Sue.

Read

Look up Romans 10:13–21; 2 Corinthians 5:14–21; 1 Peter 3:15–16. What is God saying to you about your responsibility to share the gospel?

Recount

Think back to a time when God led you to share the gospel and you obeyed. Who might need to hear the story of your obedience?

Respond

Holy Spirit, thank you for the opportunity to speak the good news to someone who might not have heard otherwise. I pray that the seeds planted in her heart would grow and that she would not forget the truth I shared with her. Thank you for others who have watered that seed. I thank you that my job is to preach and that your job is to save. At times, Lord, it is hard to open my mouth and speak. Please help me recognize and take every opportunity to speak the good news so that others may believe.

69

Life a Gardenia

God Builds His Kingdom

They will be called oaks of righteousness,
a planting of the Lord for the display of his splendor.
Isaiah 61:3

I love gardenias, particularly for their amazing aroma, but also because my childhood home had a beautiful, prolific gardenia tree in the front yard. I admire the pure white blossoms accented by deep green, glossy leaves, so I planted two small bushes in my front yard when we moved to the tropical island.

Within a couple of weeks, to my great disappointment, every leaf died and tumbled to the ground. All that remained of my treasured plants were dark black sticks. I thought they had died, but gradually the leaves grew back and they became healthy plants.

Though they now had leaves, they didn't flower. I noticed that other gardenias transplanted at the same time in another garden already had flowers. I saw new growth that looked like buds in formation, but they always fell off before opening.

As I observed my gardenia plants more closely, I discovered grasshoppers, fungus, and large red ants taking up residence among the foliage. I concluded that these pests must be eating or snapping off the buds.

One day I came upon a new type of insect laying little brown eggs on the backs of the leaves. I could not name the bug, but I knew it did not bode well for bloom production. So I searched for and crushed each critter and its eggs.

Finally, about two years after I had planted my gardenia bushes and months after I began waging war against the pests, I went outside, and behold, five gorgeous white flowers stared proudly at me. A few days later, there were five more.

To this day, I don't know why or how my gardenias suddenly started flowering, but I sure enjoyed the beautiful display of God's splendor (Isa. 61:3). My plants still needed constant maintenance. I routinely checked for bugs, sprayed the ants, and pruned the bushes. Even then, I did not know how or during which season the flowers would grow. That was left to the work of the "Gardener," the creator of all life.

I liken the growth patterns of these gardenia plants to the ways of the kingdom of God. God called a handful of servants—including my husband and me—to the island. At first, we all hardly survived the transplanting. Different ones dropped out along the way for various reasons. Little by little, more workers joined us, and our team grew stronger and healthier.

Then attacks came—sickness, accidents, riots, evacuations, conflict, even death—and threatened to destroy the work. Still the Word of God went forth, and "buds"—seekers of truth—emerged. Every now and then one would believe and become a beautiful flower. But mostly, they moved away, became disinterested, or were blinded by the lies of other religions.

Like my gardenia bush, we, the plantings of the Lord, learned to recognize the pests, the diseases, and the fungi that were trying to keep the people of God from producing abundant fruit. We continued to battle the pests that sought to destroy us, in hopes that someday the buds would turn into lovely flowers, the lasting fruit of a healthy tree.

My gardenia plant remained a small bush during my years on the island. It had yet to grow into a tree, producing hundreds of beautiful flowers. But while I waited for the flowers, I clung to God's promise that "My righteousness draws near speedily, my salvation is on the way, and my arm will bring justice to the nations. The islands will look to me and wait in hope for my arm" (Isa. 51:5).

Read

Find and read Psalm 1:1–3; John 15:1–8; 1 Corinthians 3:6–8. What is God saying to you about your "planting of the Lord"?

Recount

Remember and tell about a time when you knew that God was building his kingdom even when you encountered setbacks.

Respond

Kingdom builder, when things in my life appear to be dead, when seeds of ideas never grow to fruition, when circumstances and people continually hinder what I want to do, may I have eyes to see the displays of your splendor when I least expect them. Protect the fruit of your Word from the pests of the enemy, and may your kingdom come to my neighborhood and to the world.

70

Measuring Efforts

God Grants Success

Lord, save us! Lord, grant us success!
Psalm 118:25

As year after year progressed without the birth of a church, questions like the following peppered my journals:

What do you want me to do here? What role do I play?

What exactly are my strengths, and how should I use them?

Why do I fight and struggle with myself each time I go meet with someone?

Are we making any difference here?

Is obedience enough? Obedience to just follow you, to grow, to change personally? Even if we don't ever plant a church?

What is success? How do we measure it? Especially in ministry circles? Especially for those who rely on the financial support of churches and donors?

My husband and I tried to labor faithfully, but success was hard to measure. We prayed regularly for insight, for results from our efforts, for some sort of fruit. I paraphrased the words of the psalmist and prayed them over and over again:

> Answer me, Lord, when we are in distress; may your name protect us. Send us help from your sanctuary and grant us support. Remember our sacrifices. Give us the desires of our

> heart and make our plans succeed. We shout for joy over your victory and lift up banners in your name, O God. Please grant all our requests. I know you give victory to your anointed ones. You answer us from your heavenly sanctuary with the victorious power of your right hand. Some trust in chariots and some in horses, but we trust in your name, Lord our God. We rise up and stand firm. Lord, give us victory. Answer us when we call. (my paraphrase of Ps. 20:1–9)

Along the way, God reassured me that our efforts were not wasted (1 Cor. 15:58), and he graciously gave us glimpses of various ways he had used us and what he had done through us.

I created a one-year Sunday school curriculum and trained women to utilize it. One of these teachers then taught the Old Testament stories in her community, and a twelve-year-old girl believed in Jesus. I (along with others on my team) mentored Nella to shine the light of Jesus to children and families all over the island. Also, my helper began studying the Bible.

My husband taught a worship seminar and helped produce worship music in two local languages. The songs that he helped compose and record were distributed and sung in small gatherings. One Sunday school teacher I trained taught the songs to village children.

God raised up a team of national evangelists on the island and equipped us to expand their witness as we mentored and discipled them. More seeds were sown, more people began to seek God, and a few believed through their testimony.

God also worked in us. In faith, we followed God to be his presence in a hard place. We learned a new language and adapted to a foreign culture and environment. We removed rocks, tilled the soil, planted seeds, and loved people. We helped build a team that demonstrated the unity of the body of Christ to a resistant people.

I also considered what else God had done in us personally. He healed my husband. He led me into prayer and deeper intimacy with him. He protected us through the riots and sustained us in the loss of Anna and Nella. He taught me compassion and grace. His Scripture became alive to me in vivid and vital ways.

The former U.S. Director of Christar, Steve Coffey, says that

"Success is loving God more at the end of your term of service than you did at the beginning." I can testify this was true for me. After all we experienced, I was more in love with the Lord because I had come to know him better, experience his goodness and love, and therefore could trust him more completely.

Whatever success we achieved during our years overseas is best described by the psalmist: "Let them know that it is your hand, that you, LORD, have done it" (Ps. 109:27).

Read

Skim Psalm 20.
How do you measure the success of your ministry?

Recount

Ponder a time when God showed you that your work was successful. How can you make a record of this for future generations?

Respond

All Sufficient One, show me where I am defining success according to a worldly standard and not as you define it. I humbly ask that you would give me the desire of my heart and make my plans succeed. I trust in you and your power, knowing that you will bring fruit from my labors. I offer my efforts to you and trust that you will multiply and reward them as you see fit.

71

Leaving the Island

God Guides Us

Whether you turn to the right or to the left, your ears will hear a voice behind you, saying, "This is the way; walk in it."
Isaiah 30:21

During what would be our last team retreat, I sat "cross-legged on the floor in the circle of women. Looking around at my teammates and dearly loved friends, I began to weep."[60] In *Grit to Stay Grace to Go*, I describe how I did not know why, but I had an overwhelming sense that I would never again be in a room with that particular group of teammates.

Perhaps it was a reaction to my husband's "spirit restlessness," brought on by his new understanding of how God had wired him for ministry. Maybe it was because Mark's primary role of leading the national team had transitioned to a local believer, I had finished the Sunday school curriculum, and Nella (my primary mentee) was now with the Lord. Maybe it was simply that Mark had grown weary of reinventing himself in order to get a visa to remain in country.

All said, we sensed the Lord might be directing us to return to the U.S. and transition into a new phase of ministry. Of course, more work could always be done in that needy land, and we had no desire to leave our wonderful team and friends. Yet working just because it was needed and loving our team were not reason enough to stay. In order to survive and thrive, we had to remain convinced that God was still commissioning us to the work on the island.

We desired to follow God above all else, so we prayed for him to give us a renewed vision and passion to stay or clear direction to leave. We agonized over this decision during a year-long home assignment. It consumed every prayer and conversation, for we knew that whatever path we chose would directly affect our teammates and our ministry partners. And us, of course.

We began our home assignment in a depleted state and pursued God's healing. Mark engaged in personal counseling, and I joined a wives' group. Throughout the year, God revived our souls. As we turned to him for guidance, we each (separately from each other) discovered the following verses:

> I have called you back from the ends of the earth, saying, "You are my servant." (Isa. 41:9 NLT)

> "They will return from the land of the enemy. So there is hope for your descendants," declares the LORD. "Your children will return to their own land." (Jer. 31:16–17)

These scriptures and others resonated as clear responses to our request to "tell us where we should go and what we should do" (Jer. 42:3). God's still small voice (1 Kings 19:12; John 10:3–4) seemed to say, "I have called you back." We then asked God to confirm this new direction in multiple ways.

He did so by providing a way for Mark to pursue a counseling degree and receive mentoring from two local counselors. And our local church invited Mark to exercise his gifts in leading worship and me to start a women's ministry.

We also sought the advice of our mission leaders, sending church, family, and friends. All confirmed that following this new path seemed to be a logical next step. In the end, our teammates graciously released us, although our leaving created hardships for them.

As we journeyed through this grueling process, God also guided me specifically to appreciate the desires of my husband's heart (Ps. 37:4; Ps. 145:19). Knowing that Mark would now get to pursue a job that flowed from his true self and gift-mix helped me to accept this transition—even though it meant leaving my dearest friends.

Final confirmation for me came as I strolled around our town in the northeastern U.S. As I walked, I talked to the Lord: *Lord, I see a church right there. And another one. And yet another. What about the unreached? Mark and I committed to going where others would not. Why do you now ask us to stay here where a church sits on almost every block? This doesn't make sense.*

God's gentle voice answered: *Do you think I love the people on the island more than those of small-town U.S.A.? Of course not. I love all equally and know where you are most needed. I orchestrate the building of my church everywhere.*

After over a year of searching, I finally felt peace (Phil. 4:6–7) about the huge decision to return stateside. As God had guided us to Indonesia, so he led us to leave. Many unknowns and challenges still lay ahead, but I knew we followed God and that he would continue to be our guide to the very end of our lives (Ps. 32:8; Ps. 48:14; Isa. 48:17).

Read

Look up and meditate on the verses referenced above.
What is God saying to you about your own difficult decision?

Recount

Remember when God guided you through a difficult decision. Who can you tell that might need courage to take their next step?

Respond

"Teach me your way, Lord; lead me in a straight path" (Ps. 27:11). "Show me your ways, Lord, teach me your paths. Guide me in your truth and teach me, for you are God my Savior, and my hope is in you all day long" (Ps. 25:4–5).

72

Through a Young Adult's Eyes

God Sees Us and Loves Us

She gave this name to the LORD who spoke to her:
"You are the God who sees me," for she said,
"I have now seen the One who sees me."
Genesis 16:13

Experts say it's beneficial for TCKs to return to their overseas home in order to experience closure. With that in mind, eight years after we left the island, we returned as a family for two weeks. Our son, John-Mark, then age nineteen, wrote these words about his experience. I share it with his permission.

> The past two weeks feel like a dream. Like I was picked up and shot into the sky to soar through the clouds I've stared at dumbstruck and amazed for years. Like I fell asleep, cradled in the airplane wings that picked me up and let me fly, only to awake and feel so alive with a racing heart and powerful tears falling down my face. Like a sharp knife rushing through me, as I stand on a hilltop and inhale the brightest saturation of color and light and lingering smell and pounding sound.
>
> Massive wind races with gravity through the hills and trees, making palm trees bend and leaves rustle, sending gentle sounds out like great breakers smashing on rocks below. Burning coconuts wither down and lift up into the air and prickle my nose. A burning, brilliant, fiery sun shines on me from miles above, reflecting off salt, water, color, deep with greens and blues and spiked ribbons of turquoise.
>
> I saw millions of gleaming stars and a silvery Milky Way's

swirling arms scattered across the sky and the Earth turned on itself at a thousand miles an hour. And I stared, dazzled and wonderstruck, breathless at the marvelous wonder of the still, churning, sparkling, inky black universe.

It's like remembering a dream after waking up. Faded and distant, yet vivid and happening. There's a sharp sense of longing for dream to become reality, for the endless waterfall of colors, and sounds thundering off the brink of consciousness into my sleepy eyelids to never cease, and I can keep on dreaming . . .

But I'm wide awake and it's over, and I ache at this reality. It feels like a lost lover, a dead brother, a missing friend. I slowly recall the smells, sounds and colors and shapes, and find pain, loss, and loneliness. I don't know why, but I weep at the memory of it all, bitter pangs of grief flow out of eyes and form little spots on my sheets. I know something's broken, but I haven't known what to do for eight years.

I used to think my story was about a boy who left the home he loved and broke apart in a world he never knew. But I've seen the whole world again, and my eyes are open wide with beaming new perspective, like I fixed a wide-angle lens to my face and I see people for what they really are. Beautiful and broken, hoping to be fixed and desperately searching for meaning and love.

And I look down at myself and see that my story is more. My story is about a childish boy who spends his time in dreams, who is forced, kicking and screaming, to finally grow up and let go of his perfect and careless youth, embracing the man he should've been for so long. My story is about a boy who longs for his past and feels hopelessly alone as he stares, helpless and terrified, at the world in front of him, who wishes to crawl back beneath the windy, green palm tree and hide forever, who peeled off his skin and looked inside and found himself disgusted and horrified.

My story is about a boy, with a passion to do, who wants to unite the world and spread freedom love bounding to the furthest and darkest corners of the earth.

That night, on that hill, sitting underneath the universe, I prayed that God would send me a shooting star. I stared up at the galaxy with the sound of raging wind and surf pulsing through my ears, and whispered, "Amaze me," and took in a breath of fresh, salty air.

A small white line of light flashed through the stars and flickered out.

"Everything's okay. I'm here, and I love you."

Read

Meditate on Genesis 16:1–16; Exodus 2:23–25; Psalm 31:7. How has God shown you that he sees you and loves you?

Recount

Remember a time when God showed you his great love and reminded you that he saw you and cared for you. Record your story for future generations.

Respond

My God who sees, my heart was torn when I learned how our decision to leave the tropical island had affected our son. We broke his heart. But then you saw him, heard his cry, and showed him your love. Thank you for loving of our children (and us) no matter where you take us in the world.

Liturgy for Leaving

Lord, it's final. We're leaving,
leaving this team that we love
and this place we call home.

I'm anxious about all the logistics of moving,
packing, giving away stuff, selling things,
making sure we've seen everyone before we go.
I'm sad about not being with these lovely people ever again
and feel that I've disappointed them—
that we will leave a hole
which makes extra work for someone else.
I wonder what will happen to the ministries we leave behind.

I believed I would be here until I retired,
that this was my forever home, that my spouse would find his fit,
that my children would grow to adulthood on these shores.

I'm worried about repatriation and reverse culture stress,
that we won't find a new home, a new ministry,
that the children won't adjust well.

I confess the lie that you will love me more if I stay here,
the belief that I am only worthy
if I am out on the front lines among the unreached.
I confess the guilt I feel that I have failed or given up,
my desire to please others,
my fear of the future, of material lack,
of being a nomad once again, of not fitting in.

But I know wherever I go, you are with me.
As you have helped me navigate transition in the past,
you will do so again, for you are constant and faithful.
You have shown this to be your will,
so I will walk in faith not by sight.
I cast my anxieties on you, for you care about me.

You are the great provider,
you know what I need even before I ask.
You see the entire map of your kingdom,
and you choose to move me at this time to a new location.
I trust that you will bring others to continue the work in this place
even as you send me to pick up the work in a new place.

I walk in faith that this is your will.
I seek to please you only.
Therefore, when others question or judge my decision,
I know that you do not condemn.
Changing my location or my job or my agency
does not mean I have failed or given up.
My goal is still the same—to become like you
and serve you in your kingdom wherever that might be.

You remind me it's okay to grieve, to be sad.
You, too, said goodbye to those you love
when you returned to your Father's side.
Keep those who remain, Lord.
Help them continue to labor well in the task you have given them.

Amen.[61]

Epilogue

God's greatness, goodness, and faithfulness did not end when we left Indonesia. He did not forget that corner of the world. He brought other servants to continue building his church on that tropical isle. Nor did he forget us. He cared for us as we repatriated, found new ministries, and raised our sons into adulthood.

The events, crises, and subsequent lessons recounted in this book enabled us to, in turn, serve other global workers in their struggles and trials. Not a tear shed on that foreign soil was wasted, not a joy forgotten, nor a pain suffered in vain.

Now, as I anticipate retiring, growing old, and joining Anna and Nella and others who have entered the Lord's presence, these stories remind me that he accompanies me into the unknowns of tomorrow. No matter what lies ahead, I know he is good and worthy to be praised and served. Because he loves me, I can give him my devotion and discipleship. And I will keep telling about him and his works so that after I am gone, my next generation will know these same truths.

Wherever you are on your journey—just starting out as a new global worker, thick in the middle of daily struggles, looking back over your life, or knowing it will soon be over—God will not leave you. Your turbulent times will be different from mine. He will show up for you in unique ways exactly as you need him to. Look for him. Take note of his deeds. Make a record of all his wondrous works on your behalf—big and small—so you will not forget.

If you are feeling God's nudge to serve overseas, I hope my stories will encourage you to go for it. If God could use ordinary folks like my husband and me, he can certainly use you to help build his kingdom wherever he leads you. By now you know that we didn't plant a church. I didn't pray with someone to receive Christ. I don't know if the curriculum I labored over even survived or if my husband's recordings of songs still exist. We just tried to follow Jesus well. You can follow him too.

Whatever your path, be sure to tell and retell the stories of what God has done for you. Because when we stop telling them, people forget and go their own way. The nation of Israel learned this the hard way. They served God throughout all of Joshua's life, but when he and his generation died, the next one after that did not know the Lord nor what he had done for their nation. Consequently, they chose evil, forsook the Lord, and worshipped other gods (Judg. 2:7–13).

Somewhere along the way they stopped remembering and ceased telling the stories of God. Let's not repeat their folly. Instead, let's record and recount our stories so that our children, and our children's children, and their children after them will know our great God and Savior.

> Give praise to the LORD, proclaim his name; make known among the nations what he has done. Sing to him, sing praise to him; tell of all his wonderful acts. (1 Chron. 16:8–9)

Remember, "The one who calls you is faithful" (1 Thess. 5:24). Recall his good deeds and mighty acts in every moment of your life. And then find your own ways to tell your next generation.

Acknowledgments

All praise to my God for helping me recount the ways you led, enabled, answered prayer, and successfully brought me through my years overseas. You are worth it. I can only say, "Hallelujah, you did it all!"

I am most grateful to Mark for living these experiences with me, encouraging me to tell them, discussing the details with me, editing my words, and cheering me on. I love walking life's journey with you.

Thank you, Lane and John-Mark, for bearing with us as we dragged you around the world, let you stay long enough to fall in love with the place, and then tore you away. Thank you for allowing me to tell your stories and share your funny and cute anecdotes. Thank you, J-M, for sharing your two reflections and for painting the beautiful book cover. You both made our journey more adventurous and meaningful. I love being your mom and am so proud of you.

Thank you, Pam and Emery, for joining our unique family, for loving my TCKs, and enduring our weird and wacky stories. You are the most precious daughters any mom-in-law could imagine. We need you to help us continue growing.

Thank you to my many and beloved teammates for forbearing with me in my youth, for provoking me to love and good deeds, for laughing, exploring, and crying with me. Thank you for letting me tell parts of your story from my point of view. Without you, I would not be who I am today. Without you, my life would be less rich and complete.

Beth, thank you for reading my rough, rough draft, giving me such helpful feedback, and encouraging me to go on. Years ago, when you read my first set of stories, you counseled me to wait. I'm so glad you did. What you have helped me produce here is far better.

Bev, I'm so grateful you pointed me to the example of Joshua and the Israelites and gave me helpful feedback.

Lula and Kathy, you are my cheerleaders. I needed you.

Sue, Heather, Sarah, Lorrie, Craig, Steve, Elliot, Melissa, and

Amy, I so appreciate you taking the time to read this book and write nice things to motivate others to read it.

How could this book become reality without the assistance of editing, formatting, and cover design? Thank you, Elizabeth, Linda, Melanie, and Thai for your eye for detail and creative genius.

To my Hope Huddle, I am so grateful for your listening ear, constructive advice, and support.

Thank you to my readers. I pray that God's Spirit will not depart from you, and that the words he has put in your mouth will always be on your lips, on the lips of your children, and on the lips of your descendants—from this time on and forever (from Isa. 59:21).

And finally, my sweet Nora, holding you, watching you grow, and being enraptured by your eyes and smile has proven to be the motivation I needed to get these words written so that you might one day read the stories of your dad, uncle, gram, and grandad. But mostly so you would know the God who orchestrated it all and cared for us through it all.

About the Author

Eva Burkholder's experience as a third culture kid in Papua New Guinea, cross-cultural worker in Indonesia, women's ministry director, Bible college adjunct professor, and member care provider adds a global and soul-care dimension to her study of Scripture and storytelling. Through her writing, Eva invites readers to slow down, reflect, and apply God's word to life.

Eva's heart's passion is to build up God's people until they reach unity in the faith and in the knowledge of the Son of God and become mature, attaining to the whole measure of the fullness of Christ (Eph. 4:12–13). She gets excited when she can help someone discover how to internalize God's Word in such a way that they can live more wholly and discover their unique role in building God's kingdom.

To that end, Eva blogs regularly at www.evaburkholder.com (Pondered Treasures) and continues to teach and mentor women as she has done for over thirty-five years. She also authored *Favored Blessed Pierced: A Fresh Look at Mary of Nazareth* and co-authored *Grit to Stay Grace to Go: Staying Well in Cross-Cultural Ministry*.

Eva and her husband live in Texas and oversee the well-being of global workers for a church planting agency. A graduate of Baylor University (Waco, TX), she also has a Master's in Christian Education from Columbia International University (Columbia, SC).

Crafting (specifically macramé) and spending time with her two sons, their wives, and grandchildren gives life to her soul.

Connect with Eva on Facebook @authorevaburkholder, Instagram @evaburkholder, Threads @evaburkholder, and LinkedIn @eva-burkholder.

Notes

[1] Eva Burkholder, *Favored Blessed Pierced: A Fresh Look at Mary of Nazareth* (Richardson, TX: Pondered Treasures Books, 2019), 103.
[2] Burkholder, 104.
[3] See also Ps. 89:1–2; Ps. 145:4–7.
[4] Columbia International University, Columbia, SC.
[5] For liturgies on a broad range of topics, I suggest *Liturgies and Laments for the Sojourner, Volume One and Volume Two* by Alicia Boyd, Heather Fallis, and Tamika Rybinski.
[6] For creative ways to tell your story to the next generation, I suggest *A Legacy of Days* by Letitia Suk.
[7] Related scripture listed in order of appearance: 3 John 1:5–8; Phil. 1:3–5; 4:10–23; Ps. 37:25; Matt. 5:16; Eph. 5:8–10; Isa. 9:2.
[8] Eileen Crossman, *Mountain Rain* (Robesonia, PA: OMF Books, 1984), 167.
[9] Crossman, 169.
[10] *Great is Thy Faithfulness*, public domain.
[11] Erma Bombeck, *When You Look Like Your Passport Photo, It's Time to Go Home,* https://www.expat.or.id/info/ermabombeck.html.
[12] David Benner, *Surrender to Love* (Downers Grove, IL: InterVarsity Press, 2003), 40.
[13] Related scripture listed in order of appearance: Matt. 19:29; Phil. 2:9–11; Matt. 9:38; Heb. 13:5; Ps. 90:17.
[14] Simon Langton, *Pride and Prejudice*, BBC, 1995 TV series, Episode 3, 12:26.
[15] Stephanie Leigh Gutierrez, host, *7 Types of Rest Every Missionary Needs with Dr. Saundra Dalton-Smith*, season 7, episode 14, "Modern Day Missionaries Podcast," April 10, 2025, 41 min, https://podcasts.apple.com/us/podcast/modern-day-missionaries/id1650279020?i=1000702968245&r=1333.
[16] Read more about Sue in entries 27 and 68.
[17] Related scripture: Eph. 6:11–13.
[18] C. S. Lewis, *Horse and His Boy* (New York, NY: HarperTrophy, 1954), 176.
[19] Dr. Robert S. Miller, *Spiritual Survival Handbook for Cross-Cultural Workers* (Orlando, FL: Bottomline Media, 2011), 11.
[20] Related scripture listed in order of appearance: Exod. 3:7; Ps. 51:10; Rom. 8:1; Ps. 34:18; Matt. 11:28; 1 John 3:1; Gal. 5:22–23; Phil. 1:6; Eph. 2:10.
[21] Carol Dowsett, "Forbearance, a Greater Grace," *Engage,* November 24, 2018, https://blogs.bible.org/forbearance-a-greater-grace/.
[22] Leslie Vernick, *How to Act Right When Your Spouse Acts Wrong* (Colorado Springs, CO: WaterBook Press, 2001), 97.
[23] Related scripture listed in order of appearance: Job 1:21; Gen. 50:20; Ps. 46:1; Isa. 43:2; Ps. 119:28; Phil. 1:6; 2 Cor. 1:3; John 10:10; Isa. 40:31.

[24] I wrote a summary of our evacuation in *Yet We Still Hope: Stories of Courage from Women Serving Around the World*, ed. Denise Beck and Sarah Hilkemann (Velvet Ashes Publishing, 2022), 66–73.
[25] John Aglionby, "Muslim leaders back Lombok crackdown," *The Guardian*, January 20, 2000,
https://theguardian.com/world/2000/jan/21/indonesia.johnaglionby.
Seth Mydans, "Tanjung Journal; Trouble in Paradise Empties Hotels," *The New York Times*, March11, 2000,
https://www.nytimes.com/2000/03/11/world/tanjung-journal-trouble-in-paradise-empties-hotels.html.
Richard Lloyd Parry, "Muslim mobs hunt Christians on resort island of Lombok," *Independent*, January 19, 2000,
https://www.independent.co.uk/news/world/asia/muslim-mobs-hunt-christians-on-resort-island-of-lombok-5372305.html.
[26] The story of Nadeem and May's harrowing escape by hiding in a field and under vegetables is found in Caryn Pederson, *Batik, A Glimpse of the Heart* (Hong Kong: BottomLine Media, 2004), 18–19.
[27] N. Tom Wright, *Matthew For Everyone Part One* (Louisville, KY: Westminster John Knox Press, 2004), 120.
[28] Based on Mark 6.
[29] Read Isobel Kuhn's story in *Nests Above the Abyss, Ascent to the Tribes*, and *Green Leaf in Drought*.
[30] Isobel Kuhn, *In the Arena* (Singapore: Overseas Missionary Fellowship Ltd., reprinted 1984), 51.
[31] Justin Taylor, "Do the Next Thing," *The Gospel Coalition*, October 25, 2017, https://www.thegospelcoalition.org/blogs/justin-taylor/do-the-next-thing/.
[32] "Standing Firm," *Topical Encyclopedia*, Bible Hub,
https://biblehub.com/topical/s/standing_firm.htm.
[33] Based on John 6:1–14.
[34] Anna, Letter given to author at memorial service, October 28, 2000.
[35] Melissa Spoelstra, *Elijah: Spiritual Stamina in Every Season, Participant Workbook* (Nashville, TN: Abington Press, 2018), 33.
[36] Related scripture listed in order of appearance: 1 Sam. 30:6; Jer 31:25–26; Ps 138:3; Eph 6:10.
[37] "2657 *katanoeó*," Topical Lexicon. Bible Hub,
https://biblehub.com/greek/2657.htm.
[38] Lori Lipsky, "Thinking Ahead to Serve Others," in *Wit, Whimsy & Wisdom: A 12-Week Devotional to Shine the Light on God's Word*, ed. Kathy Carlton Willis and Michelle Rayburn (3G Books, 2021), 132.
[39] Eva Burkholder, "Our Mouths Were Filled with Laughter," in *Yet We Still Laugh: Stories of Humor and Hope from Women Serving Around the World*, ed. Sarah Hilkemann, Laura Bowling, and Denise Beck (Velvet Ashes Publishing, 2025), 23–28.
[40] Related scripture listed in order of appearance: Matt. 7:13–14; Rom. 8:18–39; 1 Sam. 1:7–20; Ps. 40:1–4; Ps. 94:17–19, Ps. 86; Hos. 6:3.
[41] For help on how to respond to sexual harassment overseas, see: "Raising Radiant Daughters – Part I: Dispelling The Silence" and

"Raising Radiant Daughters – Part II: Telling The Truth," *Thrive Connection*, 2003.
https://thriveconnection.com/2003/04/15/raising-radiant-daughters-part-i-dispelling-the-silence/.
https://thriveconnection.com/2003/06/01/raising-radiant-daughters-part-ii-telling-the-truth/.
[42] Eva Burkholder, "Goodbye, Dear One," *Velvet Ashes*, September 9, 2021. https://velvetashes.com/goodbye-dear-one/. Used by permission with minor edits.
[43] Related scripture listed in order of appearance: Matt. 28:5–6; Luke 24:5–8, 19–21; Isa 57:1–2.
[44] Nella was introduced in entry 42.
[45] This story is also told by Pederson in *Batik*, 55.
[46] Pederson, *Batik*, 55.
[47] Joy Ridderhoff, *Are You Rejoicing?* (Los Angeles, CA: Gospel Recordings Incorporated, 1984), day 23,
https://globalrecordings.net/en/are-you-rejoicing.
[48] Ridderhoff, Day 13.
[49] Ridderhoff, Day 21.
[50] Ridderhoff, Day 22.
[51] Ridderhoff, Day 24.
[52] Ridderhoff, Day 26.
[53] Ridderhoff, Day 27.
[54] Ridderhoff, Day 28.
[55] Related scripture listed in order of appearance: James 1:5; Col. 1:18; Eph. 3:17–19; Col. 1:9; 3:12–15.
[56] Wife of author Don Richardson.
[57] If left untreated, pre-eclampsia can develop into life threatening eclampsia.
[58] Stephen W. Smith, *Embracing Soul Care: Making Space for What Matters Most* (Grand Rapids, MI: Kregel Publications, 2006), 175.
[59] Related scripture listed in order of appearance: Ps. 48:14; Isa. 48:17; Rom. 12:1–2; Matt. 26:39–42; James 1:22–23; John 10:3–5; Ps. 119:24, 105; Acts 16:6–7; Prov. 15:22; Isa. 30:21; 1 Kings 19:12; Ps. 37:4; 145:16, 19; Phil. 4:6–7.
[60] Sue Eenigenburg and Eva Burkholder, *Grit to Stay Grace to Go: Staying Well in Cross-Cultural Ministry* (Chicago, IL: Williams Cary Publishing, 2023), xvii.
[61] Related scripture listed in order of appearance: 2 Cor. 5:7; 1 Pet. 5:7; Phil. 4:19; Matt. 6:8; Gal. 1:10; Phil. 2:5–7; Acts 20:36–38.

Made in the USA
Coppell, TX
15 June 2026

81291578R00164